PICTURE COOK

SEE. MAKE. EAT.

KATIE SHELLY

Ulysses Press

Published by
Ulysses Press
P.O. Box 3440
Berkeley, CA 94703
www.ulyssespress.com

ISBN: 978-1-61243-234-2
Library of Congress Catalog Number 2013938627

Printed in China by Everbest through Four Colour Print Group

10 9 8 7 6 5 4 3 2 1

Acquisitions Editor: Katherine Furman
Editor: Lauren Harrison
Index: Sayre Van Young

Distributed by Publishers Group West

CONTENTS

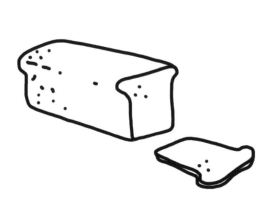

EVERYTHING YOU NEED TO COOK GREAT FOOD
IS RIGHT HERE. START WITH THE LEGEND AND
BASIC TECHNIQUES TO ORIENT YOURSELF WITH
THE WAY THIS BOOK WORKS. THERE'S ALSO A
METRIC CONVERSION PAGE IN THE BACK IF YOU
NEED IT.

AND REMEMBER—THE FOLLOWING RECIPES ARE
NOT INTENDED AS PRECISE CULINARY
BLUEPRINTS. INSTEAD THEY ARE MEANT TO
INSPIRE IMPROVISATION, EXPERIMENTATION
AND PLAY IN THE KITCHEN.

HAVE FUN & BE FREE!

-Katie

LEGEND

NO
HEAT

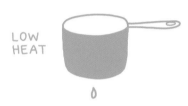

LOW
HEAT

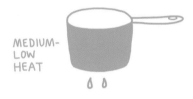

MEDIUM-
LOW
HEAT

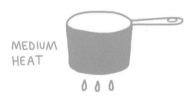

MEDIUM
HEAT

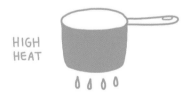

HIGH
HEAT

PREHEAT
OVEN TO
425° F

BAKE
FOR
10 MIN

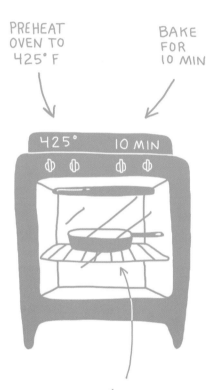

SAUTÉ PANS
IN THE OVEN
ARE ALWAYS
CAST-IRON OR
SOMETHING THAT
SAYS "OVENPROOF"

START WITH
THE LOWEST
SETTING &
WORK YOUR
WAY TO THE
HIGHEST

WHEN NO
MEASUREMENT
IS GIVEN,
AMOUNT IS
"TO TASTE"

BASIC TECHNIQUES:
MINCE GARLIC

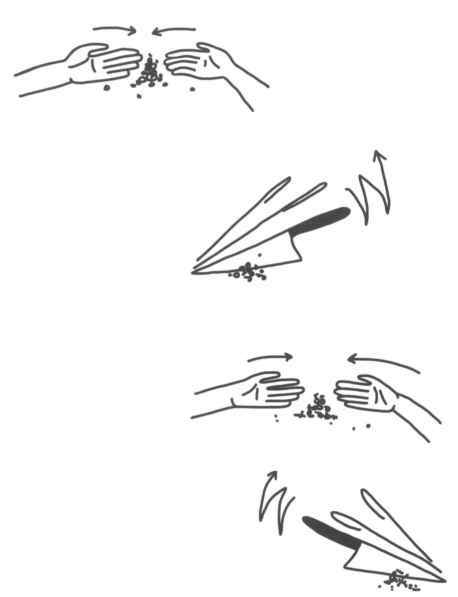

BASIC TECHNIQUES: CHOP ONION

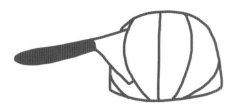

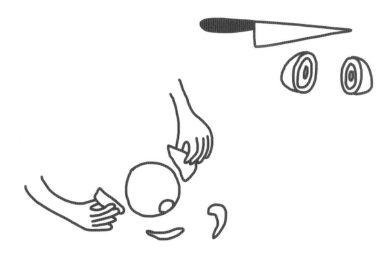

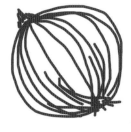

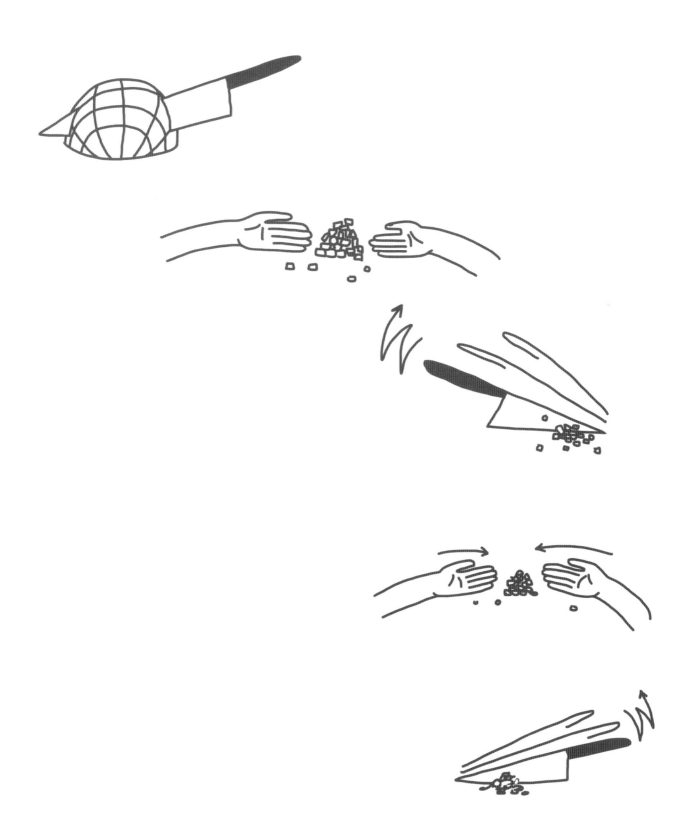

BASIC TECHNIQUES:
SLICE AVOCADO

WHAP!

WHAP!

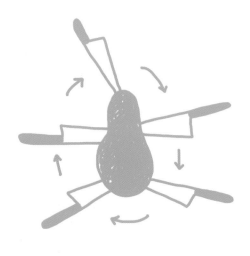

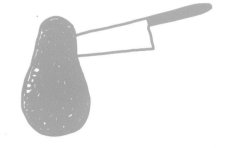

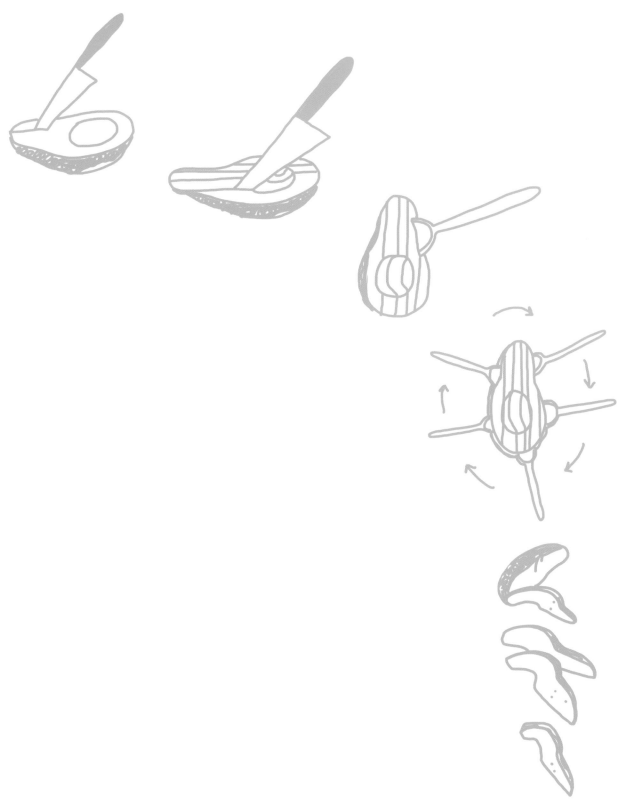

BASIC TECHNIQUES: DICE ROUND THINGS

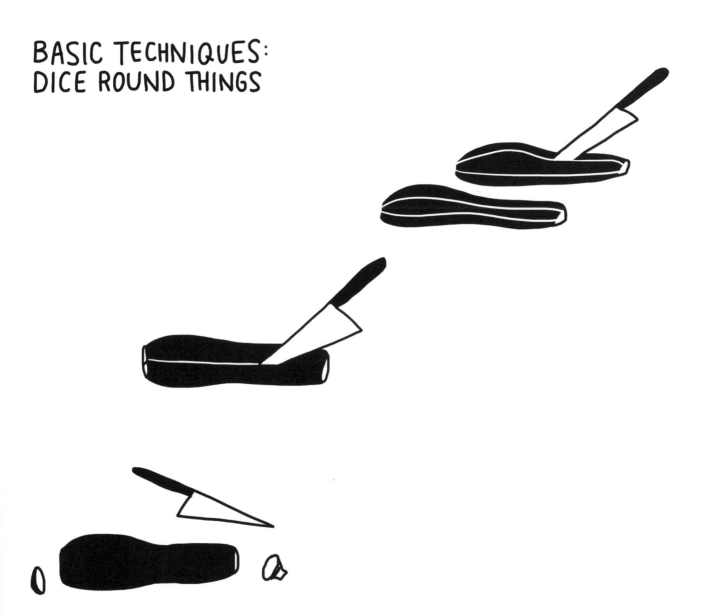

BREAKFAST

AVOCADO TOAST

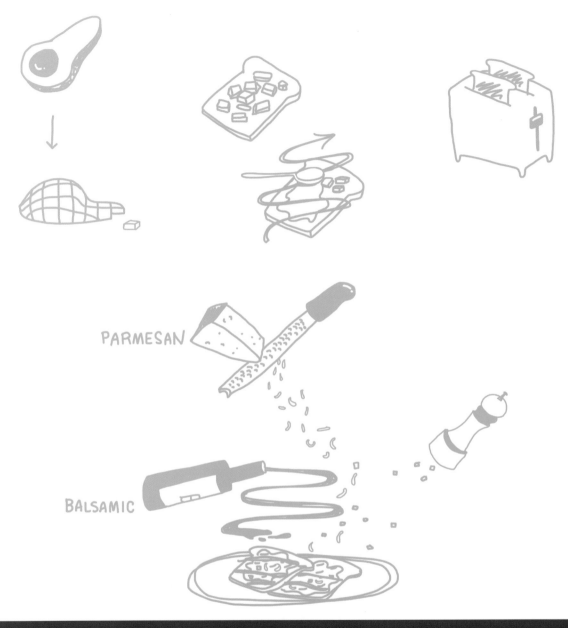

PARMESAN

BALSAMIC

 AVOCADO   ANY TYPE OF BREAD   PARMESAN CHEESE   BALSAMIC VINEGAR   PEPPER

SPARKLE TOAST

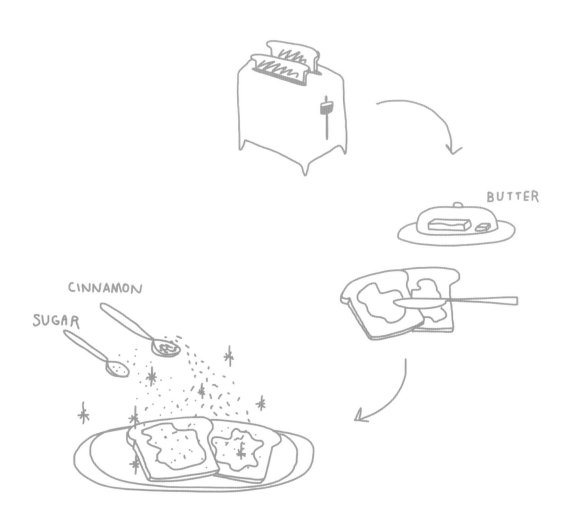

BUTTER

CINNAMON

SUGAR

ANY TYPE OF BREAD   BUTTER   SUGAR   CINNAMON

MAGIC OATMEAL

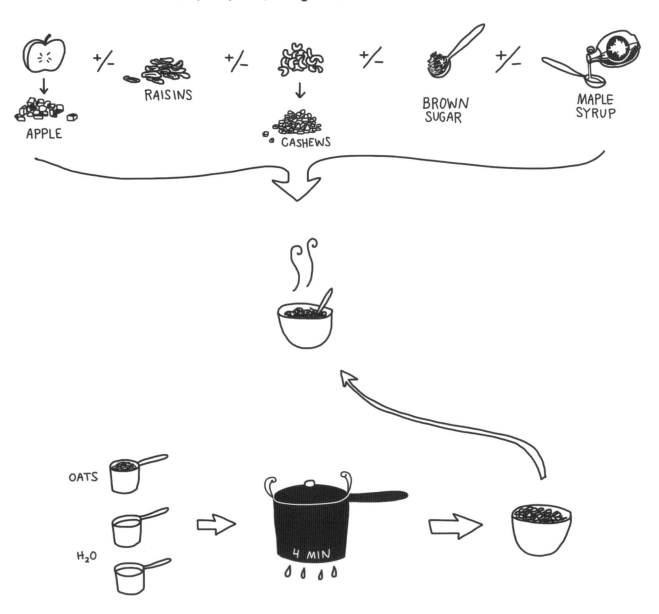

APPLE +/- RAISINS +/- CASHEWS +/- BROWN SUGAR +/- MAPLE SYRUP

OATS

H₂O

4 MIN

I CUP OATS | 2 CUPS WATER | 1/2 APPLE | RAISINS | CASHEWS OR CASHEW BUTTER | BROWN SUGAR | MAPLE SYRUP

HOME FRIES

POTATO

1/2 STICK BUTTER

CAST-IRON
OR A BAKING SHEET

350°   10 MIN

S & P

BELL PEPP

CHILE

CUMIN

PAPRIKA

ONION

1/4 STICK BUTTER

7 MIN

2-3 POTATOES,
PEELING OPTIONAL

3/4 STICK BUTTER,
DIVIDED

1 ONION

1 BELL PEPPER

1 CHILE

SALT & PEPPER

DASH OF CUMIN & PAPRIKA

THOUGHTS ON OMELETS

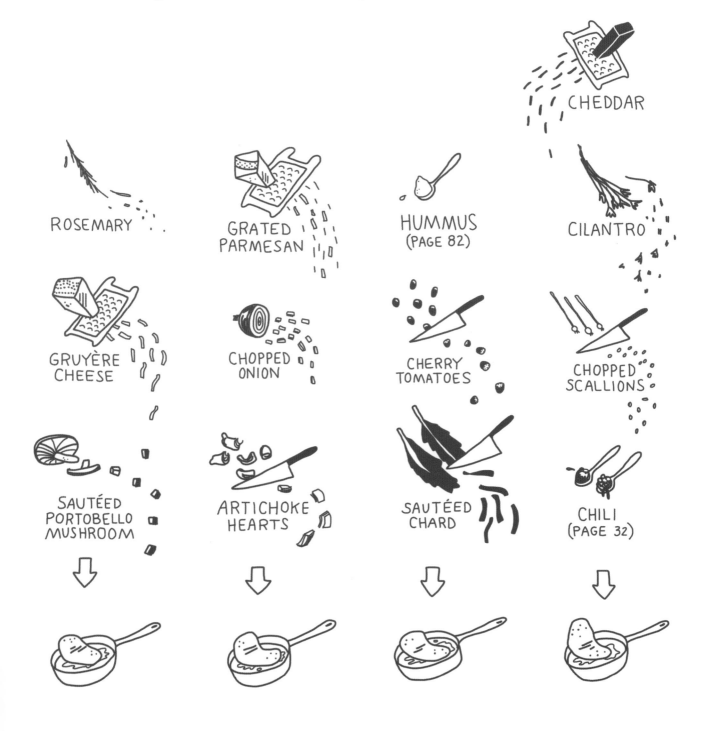

CHEDDAR

ROSEMARY

GRATED PARMESAN

HUMMUS (PAGE 82)

CILANTRO

GRUYÈRE CHEESE

CHOPPED ONION

CHERRY TOMATOES

CHOPPED SCALLIONS

SAUTÉED PORTOBELLO MUSHROOM

ARTICHOKE HEARTS

SAUTÉED CHARD

CHILI (PAGE 32)

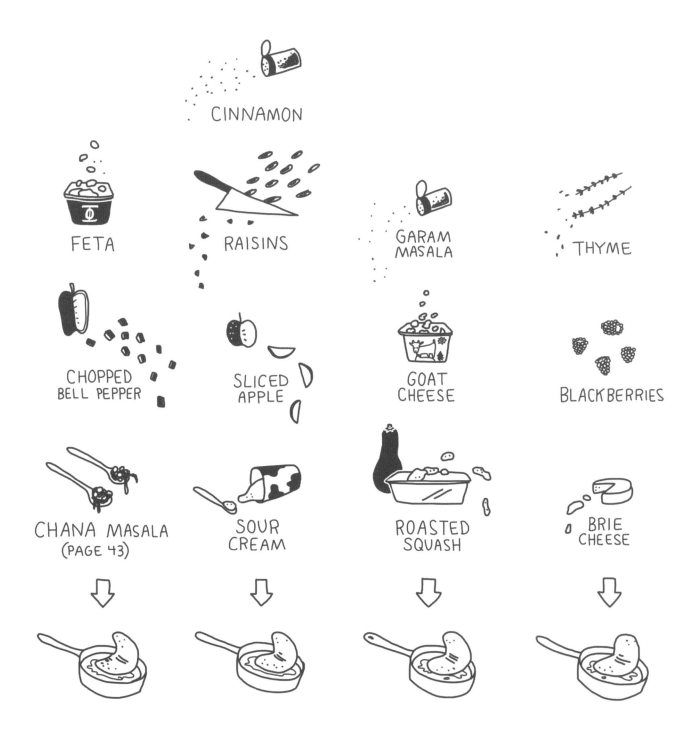

CINNAMON

FETA

RAISINS

GARAM MASALA

THYME

CHOPPED BELL PEPPER

SLICED APPLE

GOAT CHEESE

BLACKBERRIES

CHANA MASALA (PAGE 43)

SOUR CREAM

ROASTED SQUASH

BRIE CHEESE

SOUPS & STEWS

THUNDER SOUP

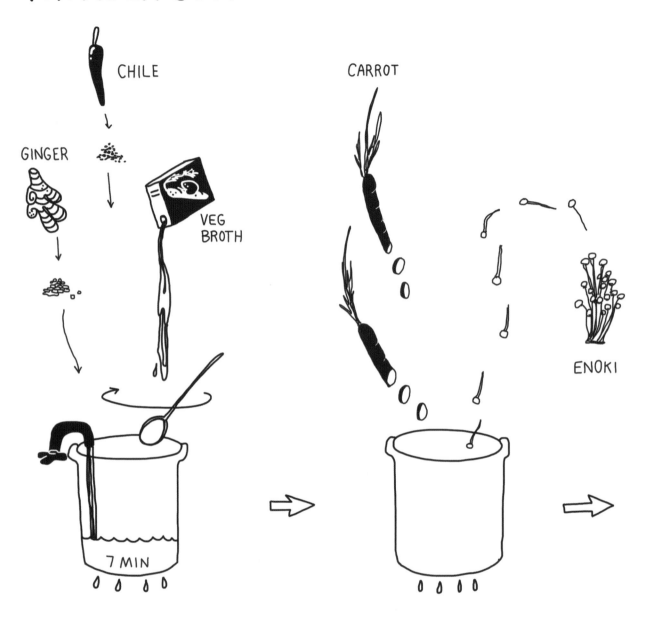

CHILE

GINGER

VEG BROTH

CARROT

ENOKI

7 MIN

ABOUT 4 CUPS WATER

1/2 CUP MINCED GINGER

1 CHILE

4 CUPS VEG BROTH

2 CARROTS

2 CUPS ENOKI MUSHROOM

OR

2 CUPS ANY MUSHROOM

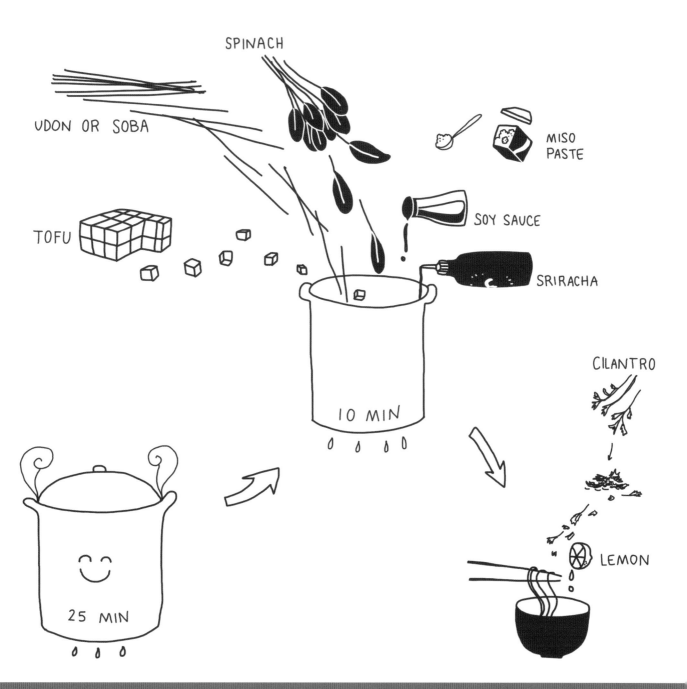

SPINACH

UDON OR SOBA

TOFU

MISO PASTE

SOY SAUCE

SRIRACHA

10 MIN

25 MIN

CILANTRO

LEMON

1 BOX FIRM TOFU | ½ BAG UDON OR SOBA NOODLE | 1 BUNCH SPINACH | 2 TBS MISO PASTE | GENEROUS SPLASH OF SOY SAUCE | SQUIRT OF SRIRACHA | HANDFUL CILANTRO | ½ LEMON

CARROT SOUP

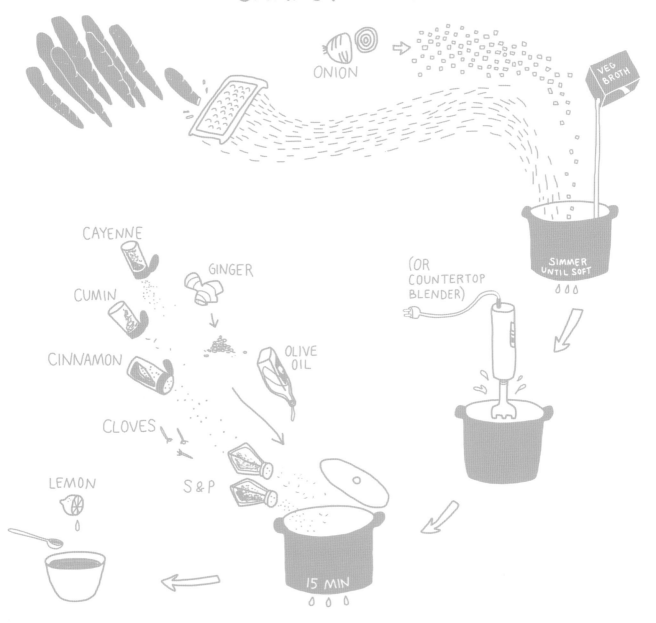

ONION

VEG BROTH

SIMMER UNTIL SOFT

(OR COUNTERTOP BLENDER)

CAYENNE

GINGER

CUMIN

OLIVE OIL

CINNAMON

CLOVES

LEMON

S&P

15 MIN

7 OR SO BIG CARROTS

1 ONION

3 CUPS VEG BROTH

1 TSP-ISH CUMIN, CAYENNE, CINNAMON

3/4 CUP MINCED GINGER

3 ISH CLOVES

3 TBS OLIVE OIL

SALT & PEPPER

1 LEMON

GAZPACHO

CUCUMBER

TOMATO

ONION

GARLIC

BASIL

OLIVE OIL

RED WINE VINEGAR

CUMIN

S&P

3 CUCUMBERS

7-ISH BIG TOMATOES

½ RED ONION

3 CLOVES GARLIC

HANDFUL BASIL

¼ CUP OLIVE OIL

½ CUP RED WINE VINEGAR

DASH OF CUMIN, SALT & PEPPER

COOL AS A CUCUMBER SOUP

CUCUMBER

LIME

DILL

JALAPEÑO

YOGURT

S&P

ICE CUBES

CHILI POWDER

3 ICE CUBES | 3 CUCUMBERS | 1 LIME | 1 JALAPEÑO | HANDFUL DILL | 1 CUP YOGURT (OPTIONAL) | HANDFUL ALMONDS | DASH OF CHILI POWDER | SALT & PEPPER

SPICY CHILI

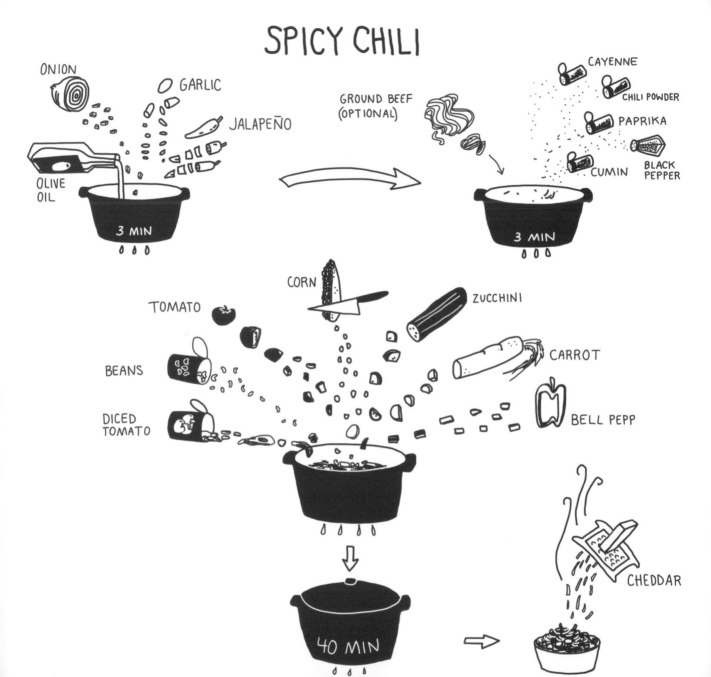

ONION

GARLIC

JALAPEÑO

OLIVE OIL

3 MIN

GROUND BEEF (OPTIONAL)

CAYENNE

CHILI POWDER

PAPRIKA

CUMIN

BLACK PEPPER

3 MIN

CORN

ZUCCHINI

TOMATO

BEANS

CARROT

DICED TOMATO

BELL PEPP

40 MIN

CHEDDAR

OLIVE OIL | ½ ONION | 3 CLOVES GARLIC | 3 JALAPEÑOS | 1 TSP EACH CUMIN, PEPPER, PAPRIKA, CAYENNE & CHILI POWDER | 15 OZ DICED TOMATOES | 15 OZ ANY BEAN | 2 TOMATOES | 1 EAR CORN | 1 ZUCCHINI | 1 CARROT | 1 RED BELL PEPP | ½ BLOCK CHEDDAR

NORTH AFRICAN STEW
ADADTED FROM NORECIPES.COM

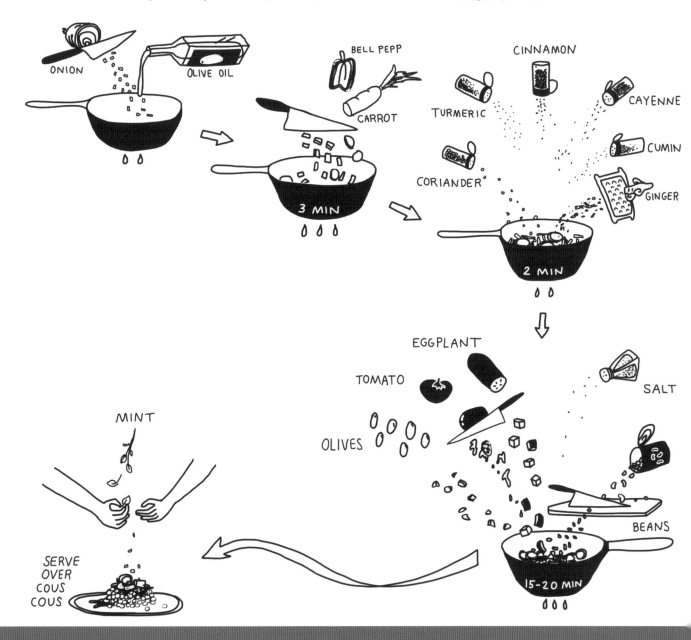

ONION
OLIVE OIL
BELL PEPP
CARROT
3 MIN
TURMERIC
CINNAMON
CAYENNE
CORIANDER
CUMIN
GINGER
2 MIN

EGGPLANT
TOMATO
SALT
MINT
OLIVES
BEANS
15-20 MIN

SERVE
OVER
COUS
COUS

OLIVE OIL

1/2 ONION

1 BELL PEPPER

1 CARROT

DASH CORIANDER, CAYENNE, TURMERIC, CINNAMON, CUMIN, SALT

2 TBS GRATED GINGER

HANDFUL GREEN OLIVES

2 TOMATO

1 CHINESE EGGPLANT

15 OZ BEANS ANY KIND

SPRIG MINT

COUS COUS

Soups & Stews 33

PHO REAL

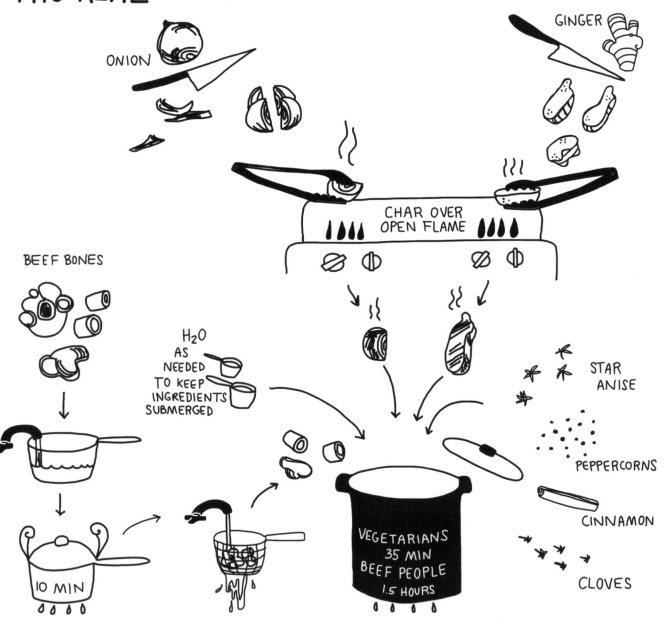

ONION

GINGER

CHAR OVER OPEN FLAME

BEEF BONES

H₂O AS NEEDED TO KEEP INGREDIENTS SUBMERGED

STAR ANISE

PEPPERCORNS

CINNAMON

CLOVES

10 MIN

VEGETARIANS 35 MIN BEEF PEOPLE 1.5 HOURS

1/2 POT WATER | 1 ONION | 1 HAND OF GINGER | 3-5 LBS BEEF OXTAIL, KNUCKLE AND/OR MARROW BONES | OR | 32 OZ VEG BROTH | ABOUT 4 STAR ANISE | ABOUT 12 PEPPERCORNS | 1 CINNAMON STICK | ABOUT 4 CLOVES

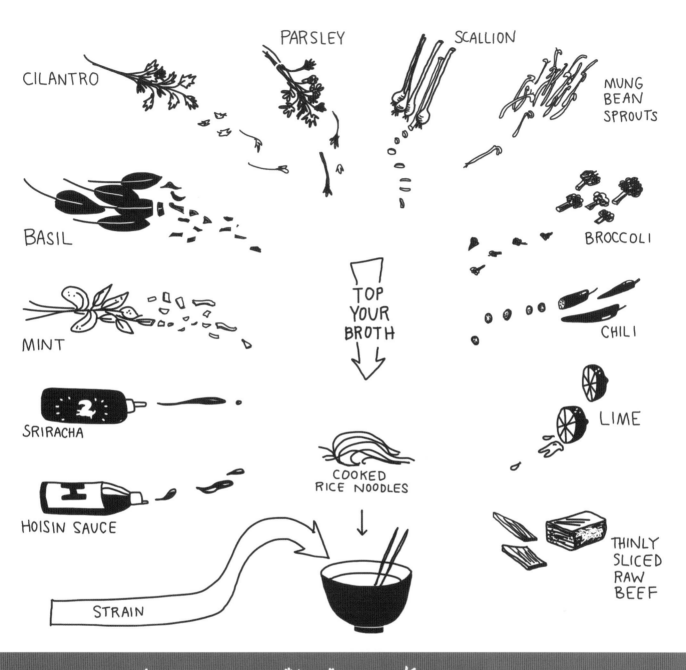

CILANTRO

PARSLEY

SCALLION

MUNG BEAN SPROUTS

BASIL

BROCCOLI

MINT

CHILI

SRIRACHA

LIME

HOISIN SAUCE

TOP YOUR BROTH

COOKED RICE NOODLES

STRAIN

THINLY SLICED RAW BEEF

RICE NOODLES | HOISIN SAUCE | SRIRACHA | MINT | BASIL | CILANTRO | PARSLEY | SCALLION | MUNG BEAN SPROUTS | BROCCOLI | CHILI | LIME | ½ POUND SIRLOIN, EYE OF ROUND, OR TRI-TIP

HEFTY MEALS

EGGPLANT PARMESAN

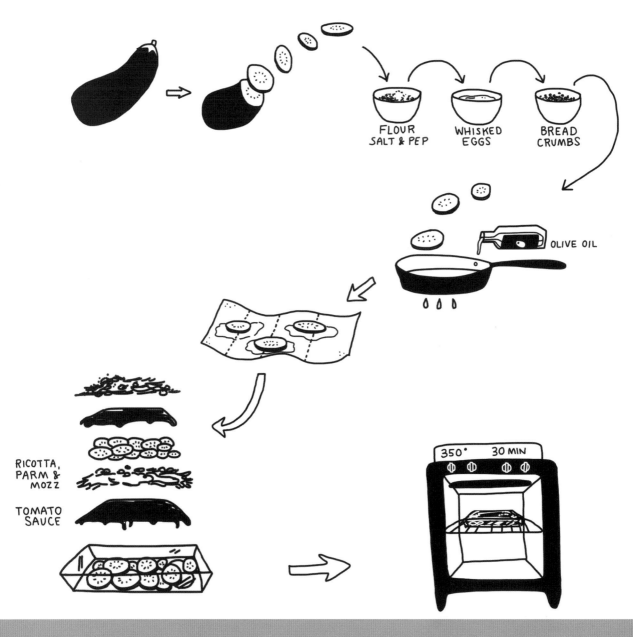

FLOUR SALT & PEP

WHISKED EGGS

BREAD CRUMBS

OLIVE OIL

RICOTTA, PARM & MOZZ

TOMATO SAUCE

350° 30 MIN

I LARGE EGGPLANT

2 EGGS

1/2 CUP FLOUR

SALT & PEPPER

2 CUPS BREAD CRUMBS

OLIVE OIL

14 OZ RICOTTA

2 CUPS GRATED PARMESAN

6 OZ SHREDDED MOZZARELLA

24 OZ TOMATO SAUCE

WHITE LASAGNA

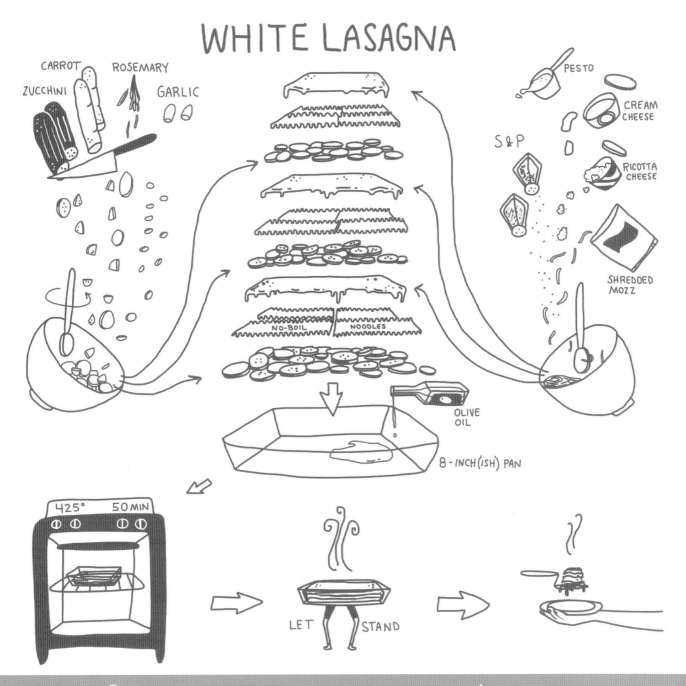

CARROT
ROSEMARY
ZUCCHINI
GARLIC

NO-BOIL NOODLES

PESTO
CREAM CHEESE
S&P
RICOTTA CHEESE
SHREDDED MOZZ

OLIVE OIL

8-INCH(ISH) PAN

425°   50 MIN

LET STAND

2 ZUCCHINI

2 CARROTS

1 SPRIG ROSEMARY

2 CLOVES GARLIC

1 CUP PESTO (OPTIONAL)

7 OZ CREAM CHEESE

14 OZ RICOTTA CHEESE

2 OZ SHREDDED MOZZARELLA

S&P

NO-BOIL LASAGNA NOODS

2 TBS OLIVE OIL

TRAVIS'S MUSHROOM RIGATONI

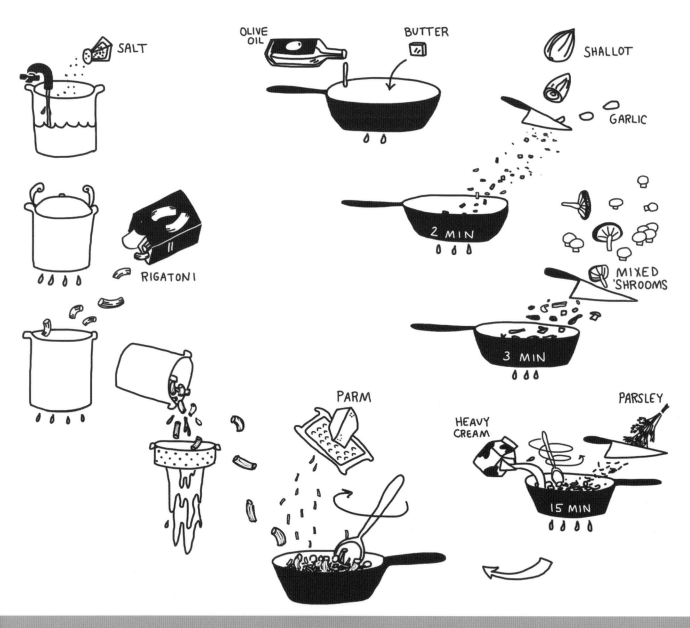

SALT

OLIVE OIL

BUTTER

SHALLOT

GARLIC

RIGATONI

2 MIN

MIXED 'SHROOMS

3 MIN

PARM

HEAVY CREAM

PARSLEY

15 MIN

3 TBS BUTTER

OLIVE OIL

2 SHALLOTS

3 CLOVES GARLIC

1½ LB SHIITAKE & CREMINI MUSHROOMS

1 BUNCH PARSLEY

½ PINT HEAVY CREAM

PARMESAN

SALT

¾ BOX RIGATONI

COMFORT POLENTA

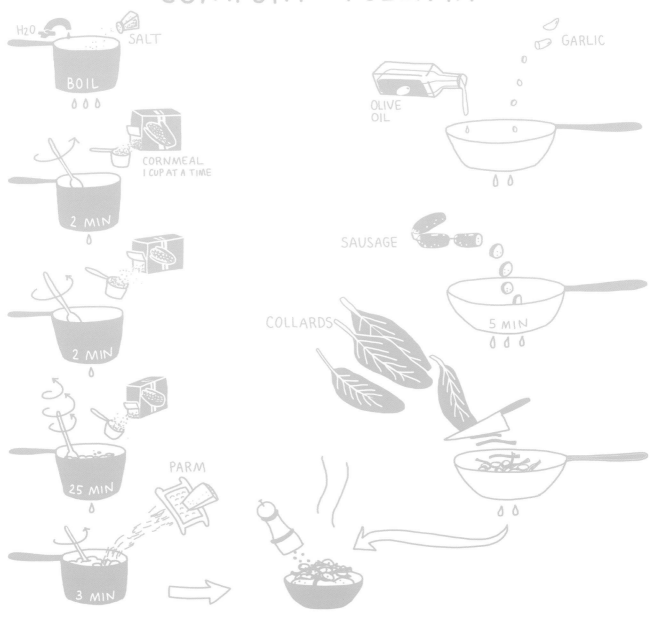

H2O · SALT · BOIL · · ·
CORNMEAL 1 CUP AT A TIME · 2 MIN
2 MIN
25 MIN
PARM
3 MIN

GARLIC
OLIVE OIL
SAUSAGE · 5 MIN
COLLARDS

  4½ CUPS H2O

 1½ CUPS CORNMEAL

 OLIVE OIL

 3 CLOVES GARLIC

 3 LINKS SAUSAGE (ANY TYPE)

 ½ BUNCH COLLARDS

 ¾ CUP GRATED PARMESAN

 SALT & PEPPER

CHANA MASALA

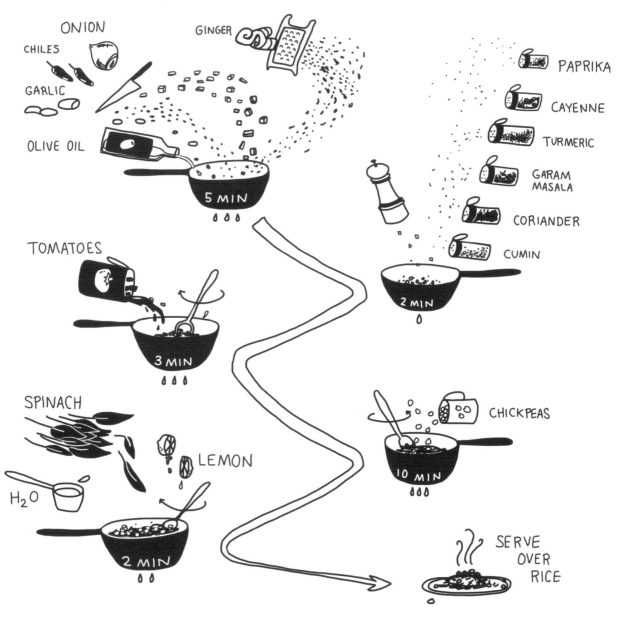

ONION

CHILES

GARLIC

GINGER

OLIVE OIL

PAPRIKA

CAYENNE

TURMERIC

GARAM MASALA

CORIANDER

CUMIN

5 MIN

2 MIN

TOMATOES

3 MIN

SPINACH

LEMON

H₂O

CHICKPEAS

10 MIN

2 MIN

SERVE OVER RICE

 OLIVE OIL 3 CLOVES GARLIC 2 CHILES 1 ONION 3/4 CUP GRATED GINGER 1 TSP CUMIN, CORIANDER & GARAM MASALA 1/2 TSP TURMERIC CAYENNE, PAPRIKA & PEPPER 28 OZ DICED TOMATOES 28 OZ CHICK PEAS 1/2 CUP H₂O 3 HANDFULS SPINACH 1 LEMON

ELABORATE FRIED RICE

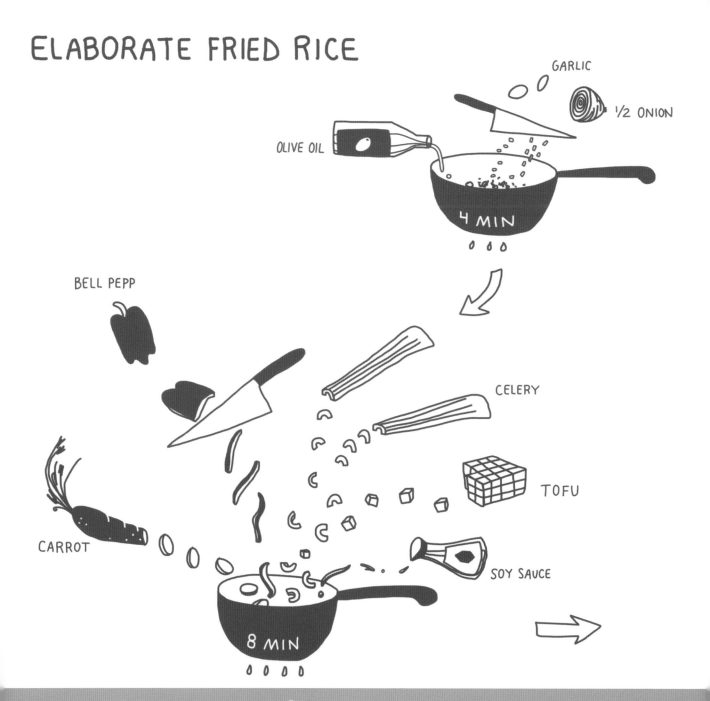

GARLIC

½ ONION

OLIVE OIL

4 MIN

BELL PEPP

CELERY

TOFU

CARROT

SOY SAUCE

8 MIN

OLIVE OIL

2 CLOVES GARLIC

½ ONION

1 BIG CARROT

1 BELL PEPPER

2 STALKS CELERY

1 BLOCK FIRM TOFU

4 TBS SOY SAUCE

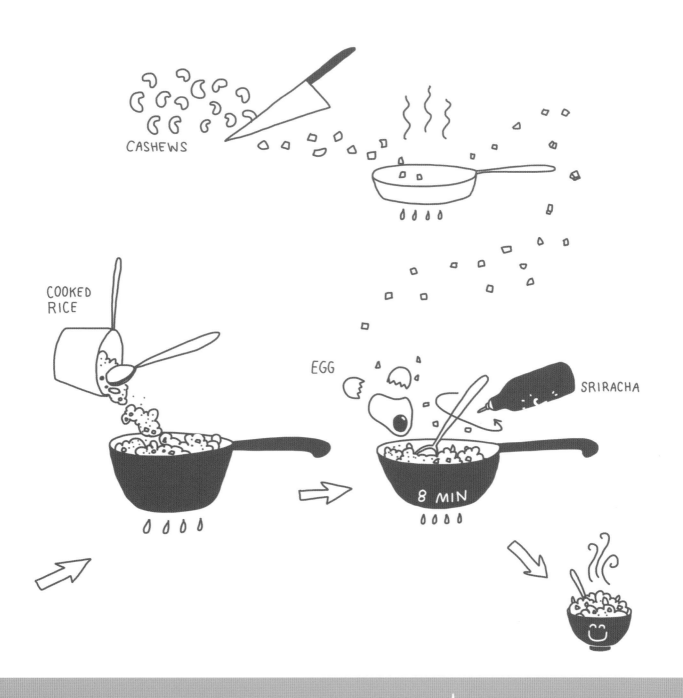

CASHEWS

COOKED RICE

EGG

SRIRACHA

8 MIN

BIG HANDFUL CASHEWS

4 CUPS COOKED RICE

1 EGG

2 TBS SRIRACHA

HUNGRY ENCHILADAS
ADAPTED FROM ANNIE'S EATS

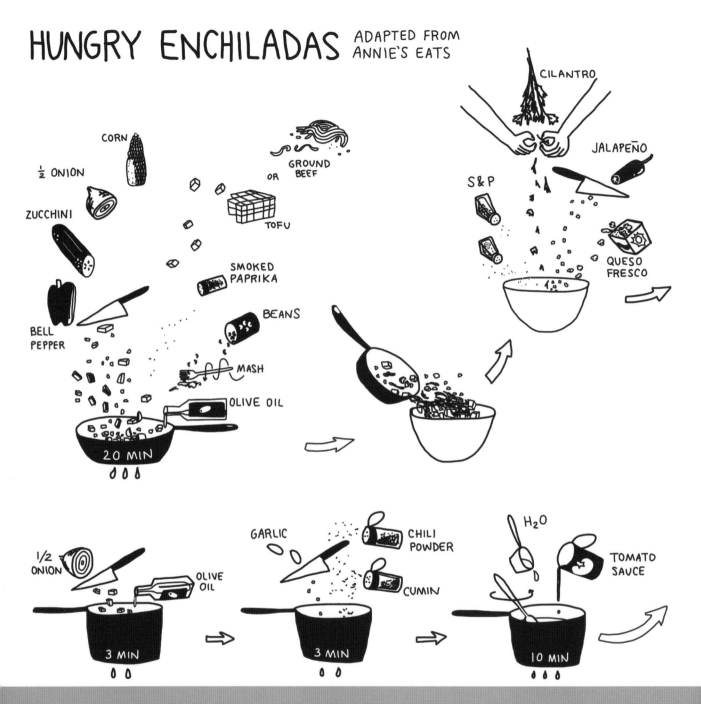

CILANTRO

JALAPEÑO

S & P

QUESO FRESCO

½ ONION

CORN

GROUND BEEF

OR

TOFU

ZUCCHINI

SMOKED PAPRIKA

BEANS

MASH

BELL PEPPER

OLIVE OIL

20 MIN

½ ONION

OLIVE OIL

3 MIN

GARLIC

CHILI POWDER

CUMIN

3 MIN

H₂O

TOMATO SAUCE

10 MIN

OLIVE OIL | ½ BELL PEPPER | ½ ZUCCHINI | 1 ONION | 1 EAR OR CAN OF CORN | DASH SMOKED PAPRIKA | ½ LB GROUND BEEF OR TOFU/SEITAN | 15 OZ BLACK BEANS | SALT & PEPPER | 1 BUNCH CILANTRO

TORTILLAS

CHEDDAR

450° 15 MIN

LIME

CILANTRO

1
JALAPEÑO

1 CUP
QUESO
FRESCO

½ TSP EACH
CHILI POWDER &
CUMIN

2 CLOVES
GARLIC

1 CUP
H_2O

15 OZ
TOMATO
SAUCE

12 6-INCH
TORTILLAS

½ BLOCK
CHEDDAR

1 LIME

THOUGHTS ON TACOS

CHEDDAR

QUESO
FRESCO

RED
ONION

RED
CABBAGE

RADISH &
SCALLION

LIME

RAZOR THIN
APPLE SLICES

BLACK
BEANS

ROASTED
BUTTERNUT
SQUASH

DICED
MUSHROOM

FRIED
EGG

SAUTÉED
SEITAN OR
SHREDDED
PORK

DICED TOFU
OR CHICKEN
SAUTÉED WITH
CURRY POWDER

KIMCHI

SAUTÉED
CHORIZO

SOFT
FLOUR
TORTILLA

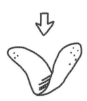

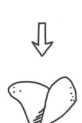

LIME

RED ONION

GUACAMOLE

MANGO

PEANUT

JALAPEÑO

SAUTÉED CORN

ARUGULA

CILANTRO

LETTUCE

CUCUMBER

QUINOA

GRAPEFRUIT

PINEAPPLE

FRIED SWEET
PLANTAINS

CHUNKS OF
COOKED LOBSTER OR
GRILLED SHRIMP

GRILLED
FISH

BACON

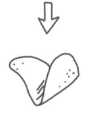

SIDES & SALADS

ANNIE'S MASHED POTATOES

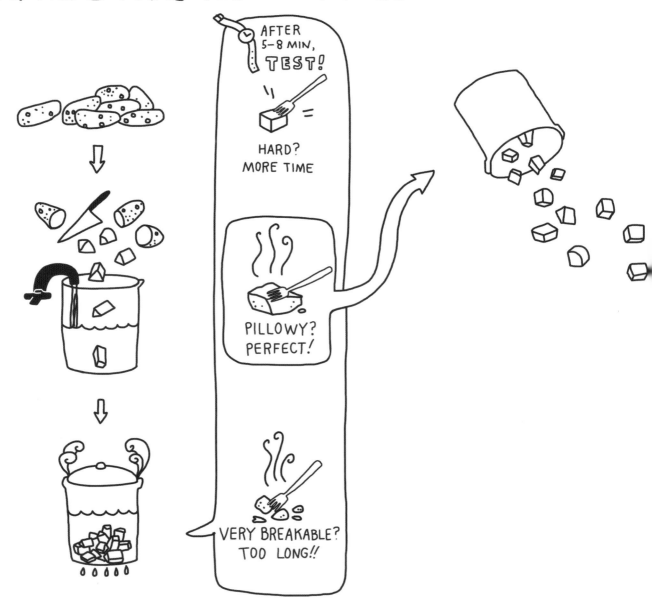

AFTER 5–8 MIN, TEST!

HARD? MORE TIME

PILLOWY? PERFECT!

VERY BREAKABLE? TOO LONG!!

5 LBS POTATOES
PEELED OR UNPEELED, UP TO YOU.

SALT

BUTTER

MILK

CREAM

DRAIN
VERY
WELL!

1 STICK
BUTTER

1/4 CUP WHOLE MILK
AT ROOM TEMP

1/4 CUP CREAM
AT ROOM TEMP

SALT
TO TASTE

NUTTY QUINOA

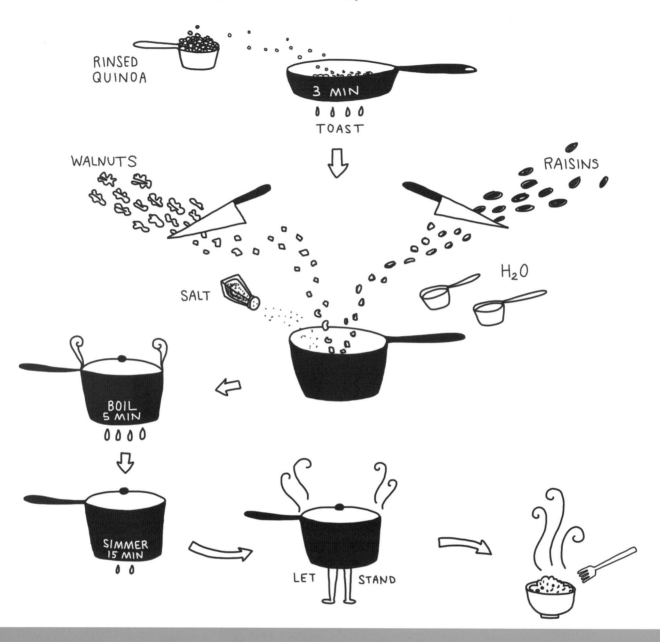

RINSED QUINOA

3 MIN TOAST

WALNUTS

RAISINS

SALT

H_2O

BOIL 5 MIN

SIMMER 15 MIN

LET STAND

 2 CUPS H_2O

 3/4 CUP WALNUTS

 3/4 CUP RAISINS

 1 CUP QUINOA

 DASH OF SALT

SUCCOTASH

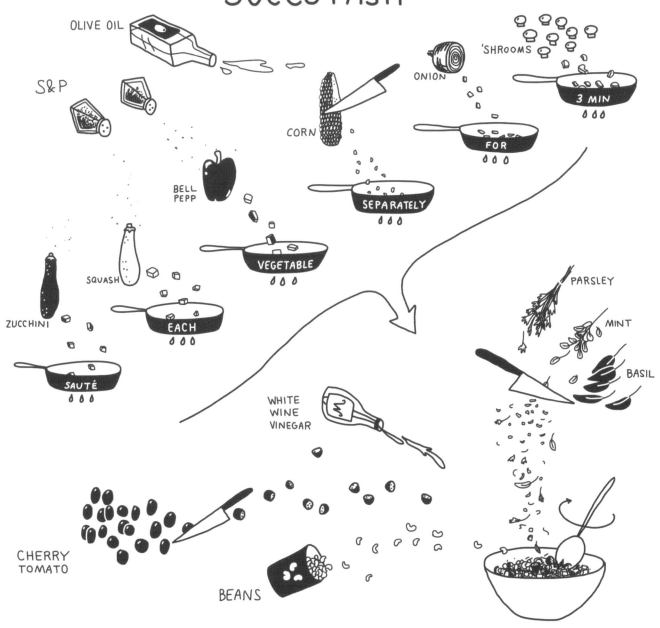

OLIVE OIL

S&P

CORN

ONION

'SHROOMS

3 MIN

FOR

SEPARATELY

BELL PEPP

VEGETABLE

SQUASH

PARSLEY

MINT

BASIL

ZUCCHINI

EACH

SAUTÉ

WHITE WINE VINEGAR

CHERRY TOMATO

BEANS

½ ONION | 1 ZUCCHINI | 1 YELLOW SQUASH | 1 BELL PEPP | 1 EAR CORN | 1 CUP MUSHROOMS | 2 CUPS CHERRY TOMATO | HANDFUL BASIL | HANDFUL PARSLEY | HANDFUL MINT | 1 CUP WHITE WINE VINEGAR | 15 OZ BEANS ANY KIND

AUNT ANN'S AMBROSIA

PINEAPPLE PECANS

NUTMEG

MINI MARSHMALLOWS

CLEMENTINE

SHREDDED COCONUT

GRAPES

MARASCHINO CHERRIES

PEAR

WHIPPED CREAM

LET STAND   ONE HOUR

| 1 CUP GRAPES | 3 CLEMENTINES | 1 CUP PINEAPPLE | 1 PEAR | 1/2 CUP PECANS | 2 TSP NUTMEG | 2 CUPS MINI MARSHMALLOWS | 2 CUPS SHREDDED COCONUT | ABOUT 10 MARASCHINO CHERRIES | 1 CUP WHIPPED CREAM |

OR

JOSÉ'S RICE

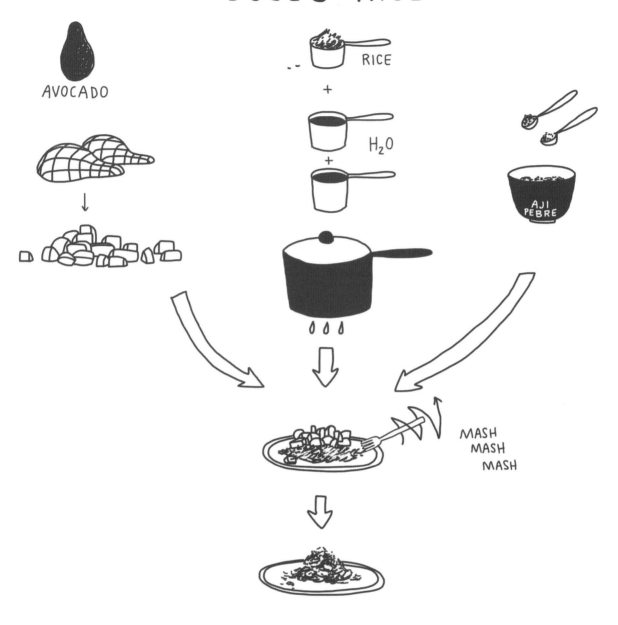

AVOCADO

RICE

+

H_2O

+

AJI PEBRE

MASH
MASH
MASH

1 AVOCADO   1 CUP RICE   2 CUPS   2 TBS AJI PEBRE
             (UNCOOKED) H_2O (SEE PAGE 80)

SQUASH MEDALLIONS

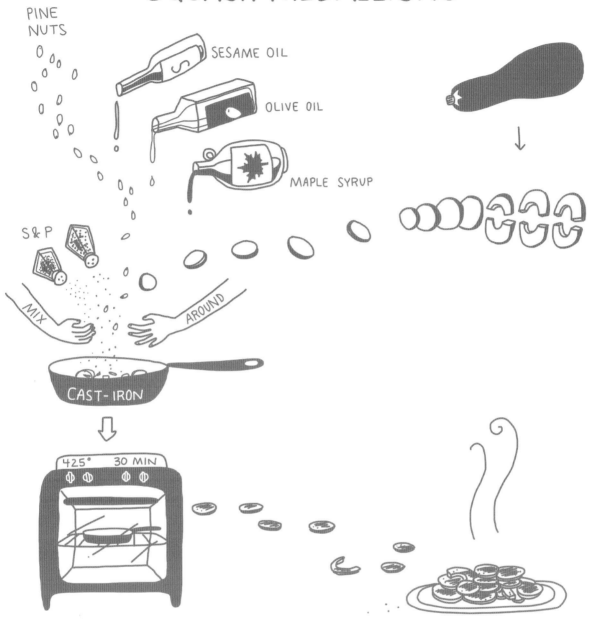

PINE NUTS

SESAME OIL

OLIVE OIL

MAPLE SYRUP

S & P

MIX

AROUND

CAST-IRON

425°   30 MIN

1 TSP OLIVE OIL

2 TBS SESAME OIL

2 TBS MAPLE SYRUP

ANY TYPE OF WINTER SQUASH

HANDFUL OF PINE NUTS

SALT & PEPPER

AURORA'S ARUGULA SALAD

BALSAMIC VINEGAR

OLIVE OIL

PECANS

1 MIN

GORGONZOLA

STRAWBERRIES

 OLIVE OIL

 BALSAMIC VINEGAR

 5 HANDFULS ARUGULA

 10 OR SO STRAWBERRIES

 HANDFUL GORGONZOLA CHEESE

 BIG HANDFUL PECANS

CHELSEA'S KALE SALAD

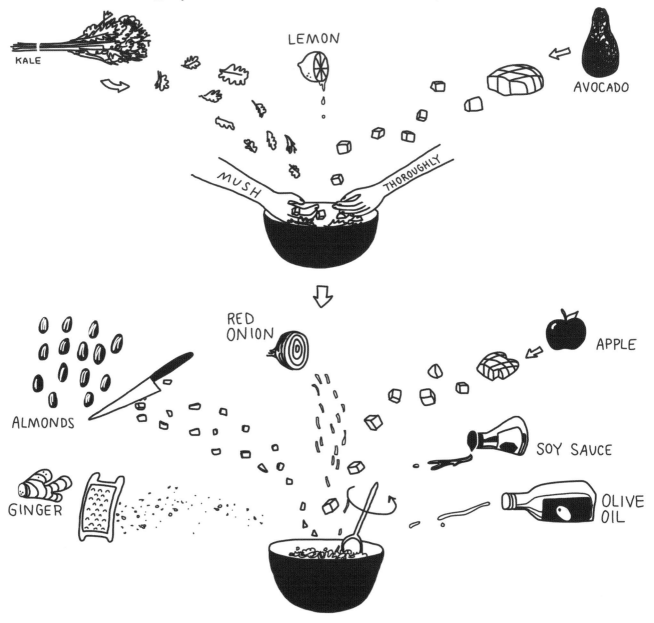

KALE
LEMON
AVOCADO

MUSH   THOROUGHLY

ALMONDS
RED ONION
APPLE
SOY SAUCE
GINGER
OLIVE OIL

½ BUNCH KALE | ½ LEMON | 1 AVOCADO | 4 TBS GINGER | BIG HANDFUL ALMONDS | ⅓ RED ONION | ANY TYPE OF APPLE | 2 TBS SOY SAUCE | 1 TBS OLIVE OIL

PANZANELLA

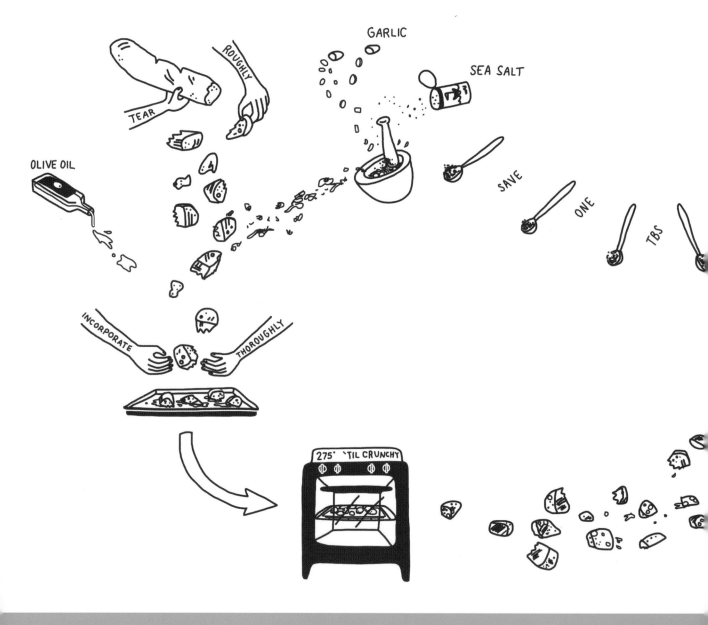

TEAR

ROUGHLY

OLIVE OIL

GARLIC

SEA SALT

SAVE

ONE

TBS

INCORPORATE

THOROUGHLY

275° 'TIL CRUNCHY

OLIVE OIL

DAY-OLD BAGUETTE

4 CLOVES GARLIC

SEA SALT

1 CUCUMBER

2 SHALLOTS

4 TOMATOES

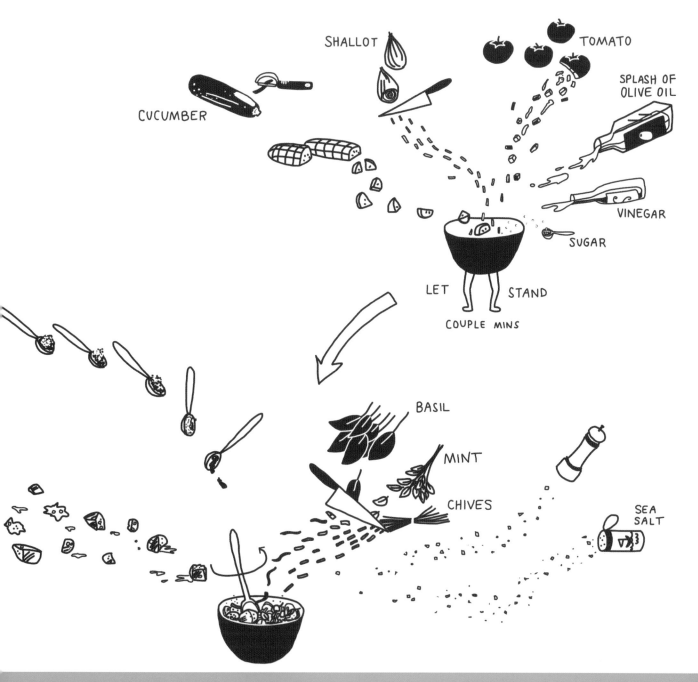

CUCUMBER

SHALLOT

TOMATO

SPLASH OF OLIVE OIL

VINEGAR

SUGAR

LET STAND

COUPLE MINS

BASIL

MINT

CHIVES

SEA SALT

 SHERRY OR CIDER VINEGAR

 PINCH SUGAR

 HANDFUL BASIL

 HANDFUL MINT

 HANDFUL CHIVES

PEPPER

FAST SNACKS

MOM'S AVOCADO & FETA SNACK

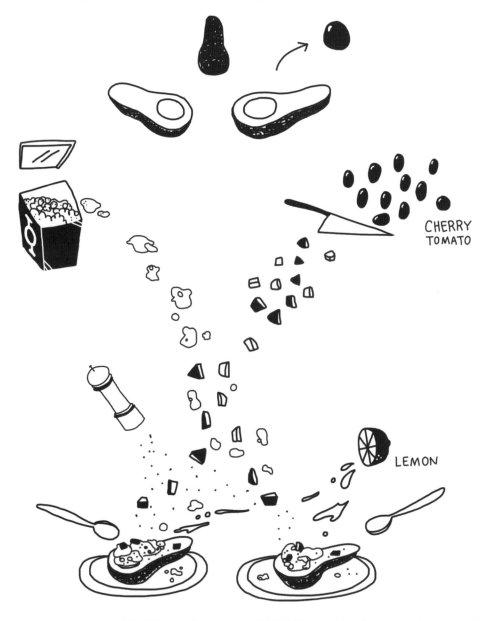

CHERRY TOMATO

LEMON

½ AVOCADO PER SNACKER | HANDFUL CHERRY TOMATOES | ½ LEMON | HANDFUL FETA | PEPPER

ENDIVE, HONEY & GOAT CHEESE SNACK

**2 ENDIVES
PER SNACKER**

**HANDFUL
GOAT CHEESE**

HONEY

THOUGHTS ON PIZZA

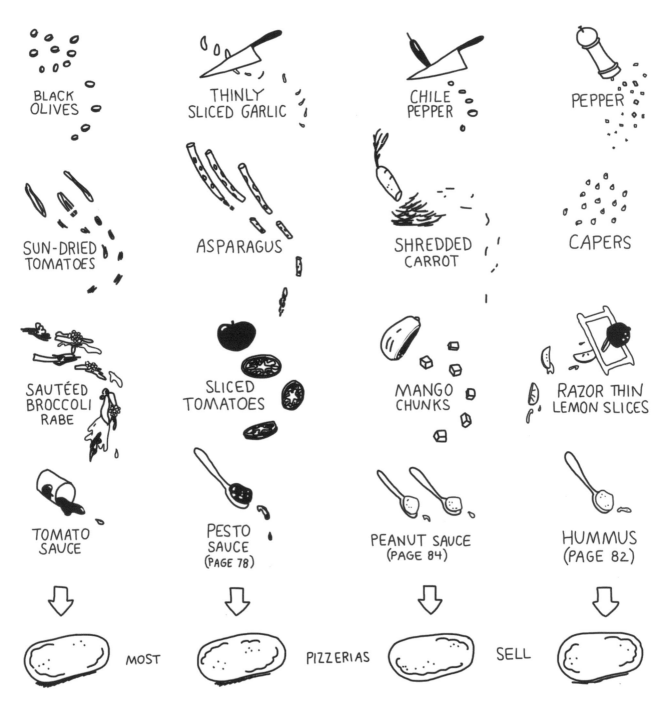

BLACK OLIVES

THINLY SLICED GARLIC

CHILE PEPPER

PEPPER

SUN-DRIED TOMATOES

ASPARAGUS

SHREDDED CARROT

CAPERS

SAUTÉED BROCCOLI RABE

SLICED TOMATOES

MANGO CHUNKS

RAZOR THIN LEMON SLICES

TOMATO SAUCE

PESTO SAUCE (PAGE 78)

PEANUT SAUCE (PAGE 84)

HUMMUS (PAGE 82)

MOST

PIZZERIAS

SELL

CHOPPED WALNUTS

LEMON JUICE

BACON BITS

FETA

CAYENNE

ARUGULA (ADD AFTER BAKING)

BALSAMIC VINEGAR

PEAR SLICES

GOAT CHEESE

SHAVED PARMESAN

SLICED FIGS

CARAMELIZED ONIONS

APPLE SLICES

CAULIFLOWER

HALOUMI CHEESE

SESAME OIL

HONEY

THEIR PIZZA DOUGH!

STRAWBERRY, HONEY & BASIL SNACK

HANDFUL
STRAWBERRIES

SEA
SALT

HONEY
(PREFERABLY RAW)

HANDFUL
FRESH BASIL

KRISPY KALE

S & P

OLIVE OIL

CAST-IRON

400°   10 MIN

2 HANDFULS
KALE

SALT &
PEPPER

1 TBS
OLIVE OIL

SWEET POTATO FRIES

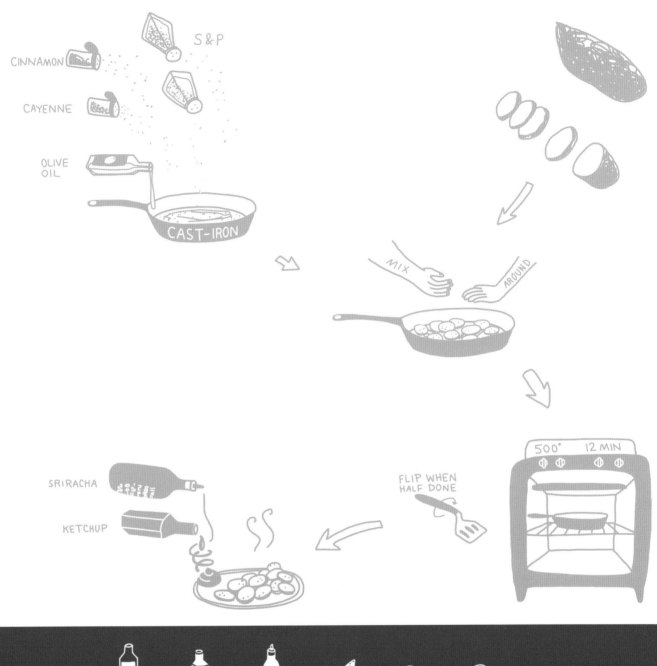

CINNAMON

S & P

CAYENNE

OLIVE OIL

CAST-IRON

MIX AROUND

500° 12 MIN

FLIP WHEN HALF DONE

SRIRACHA

KETCHUP

2 TBS OLIVE OIL

KETCHUP

SRIRACHA

1 SWEET POTATO

1 TSP CAYENNE

1 TSP CINNAMON

SALT & PEPPER

SAUCES & DIPS

ZINGY TOMATO SAUCE

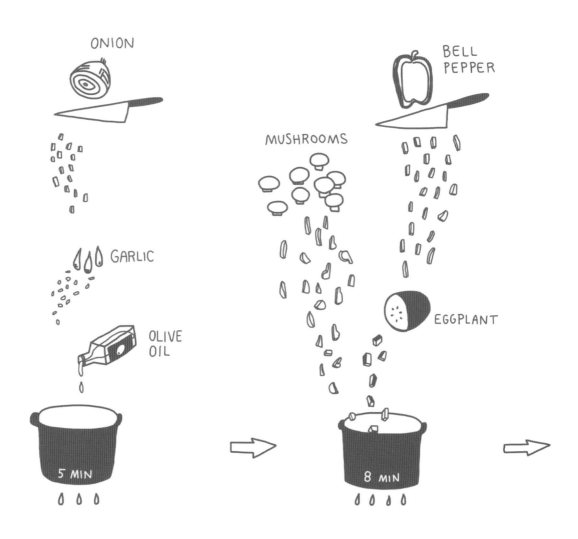

ONION

GARLIC

OLIVE OIL

5 MIN

MUSHROOMS

BELL PEPPER

EGGPLANT

8 MIN

 OLIVE OIL

 3 CLOVES GARLIC

 ½ ONION

  2 CUPS MUSHROOMS

 ½ BELL PEPPER

 ½ EGGPLANT

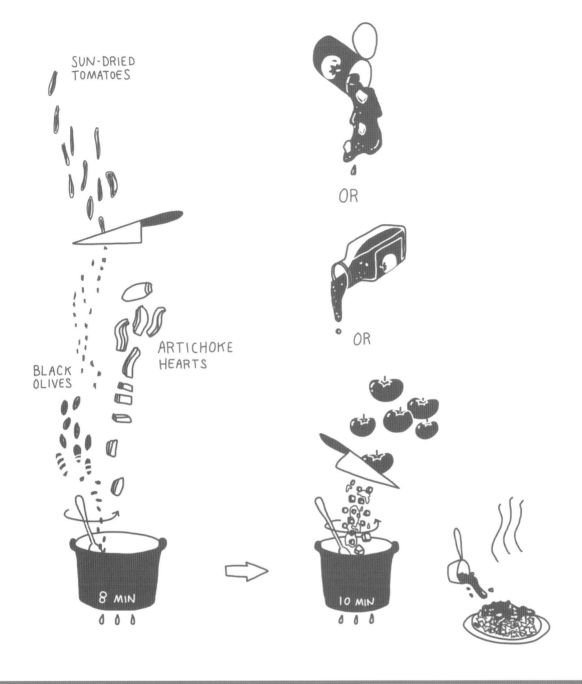

SUN-DRIED TOMATOES

OR

BLACK OLIVES

ARTICHOKE HEARTS

OR

8 MIN

10 MIN

HANDFUL
SUN-DRIED
TOMATOES

HANDFUL
ARTICHOKE
HEARTS

HANDFUL
BLACK
OLIVES

1 LB
TOMATOES

OR

16 OZ
DICED
TOMATOES

OR

16 OZ
TOMATO
SAUCE

PESTO SAUCE

BASIL

PINE NUTS

GARLIC

PARMESAN

OLIVE OIL

H_2O

5 HANDFULS BASIL

1 CUP PINE NUTS

3 CLOVES GARLIC

2 CUPS PARMESAN

3 TBS OLIVE OIL

SPLASH H_2O

PEPPER

YOU CAN MAKE SO MANY
VARIATIONS OF PESTO.

INSTEAD OF BASIL, TRY SPINACH,
NETTLES, ARUGULA OR RADISH GREENS.

INSTEAD OF PINE NUTS,
TRY PISTACHIOS, WALNUTS,
PUMPKIN SEEDS OR CASHEWS.

AJI PEBRE

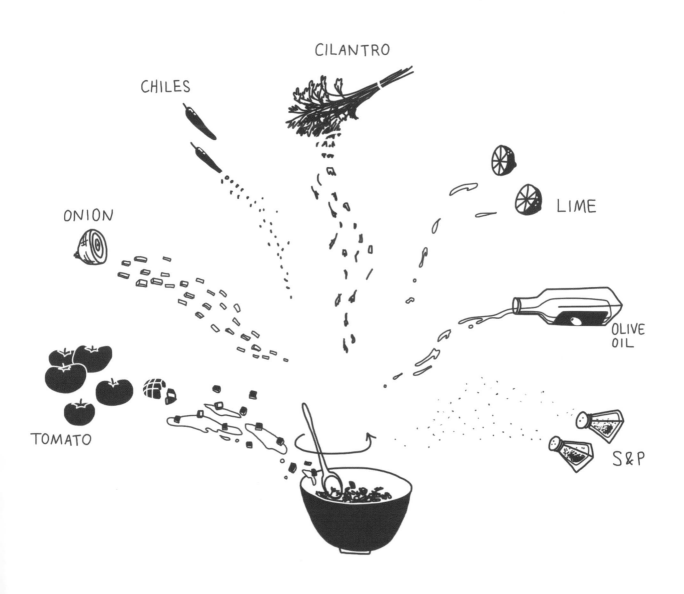

CILANTRO

CHILES

ONION

TOMATO

LIME

OLIVE OIL

S&P

8 OR SO TOMATOES — 1/4 YELLOW ONION — 2 HOT CHILES — 1 BUNCH CILANTRO — 2 LIMES — 3 TBS OLIVE OIL — SALT & PEPPER

NICK'S SALSA VERDE

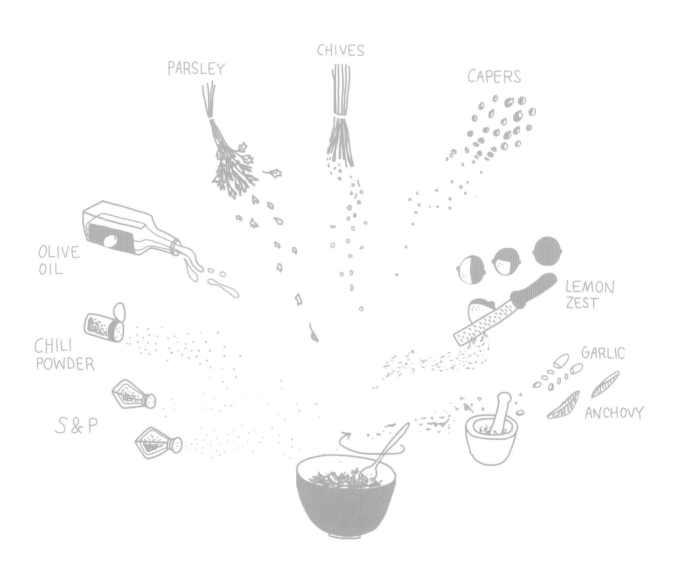

PARSLEY

CHIVES

CAPERS

OLIVE OIL

LEMON ZEST

CHILI POWDER

GARLIC

ANCHOVY

S & P

SALT & PEPPER

DASH OF CHILI POWDER

2 TBS OLIVE OIL

HANDFUL PARSLEY

HANDFUL CHIVES

ABOUT 20 CAPERS

ZEST OF 4 LEMONS

2 CLOVES GARLIC

2 ANCHOVY FILLETS

RUSTIC HUMMUS

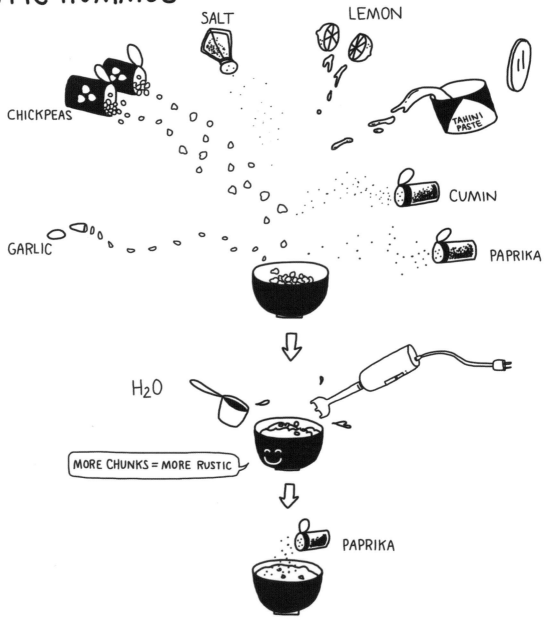

CHICKPEAS

SALT

LEMON

TAHINI PASTE

CUMIN

PAPRIKA

GARLIC

H₂O

MORE CHUNKS = MORE RUSTIC

PAPRIKA

1 CLOVE GARLIC	30 OZ CHICKPEAS, RINSED	SALT	1 LEMON	1 CUP TAHINI PASTE	DASH OF CUMIN	2 DASHES PAPRIKA, DIVIDED	BIG SPLASH H₂O

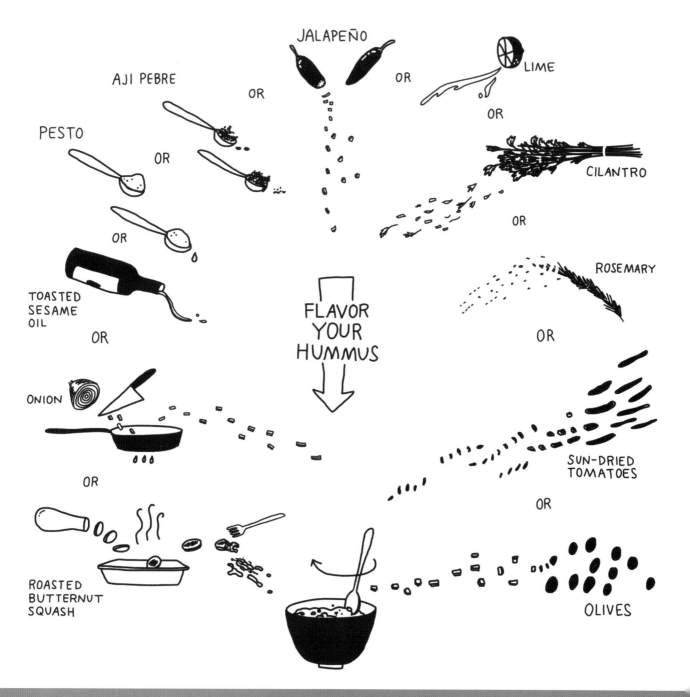

JALAPEÑO

OR

LIME

OR

AJI PEBRE

OR

PESTO

OR

CILANTRO

OR

TOASTED SESAME OIL

OR

ROSEMARY

OR

FLAVOR YOUR HUMMUS

ONION

OR

SUN-DRIED TOMATOES

OR

ROASTED BUTTERNUT SQUASH

OLIVES

BUTTERNUT SQUASH | CARAMELIZED ONION | TOASTED SESAME OIL | PESTO (SEE PAGE 78) | AJI PEBRE (SEE PAGE 80) | JALAPEÑO | LIME | CILANTRO | ROSEMARY | SUN-DRIED TOMATO | OLIVES

CHEATING PEANUT SAUCE

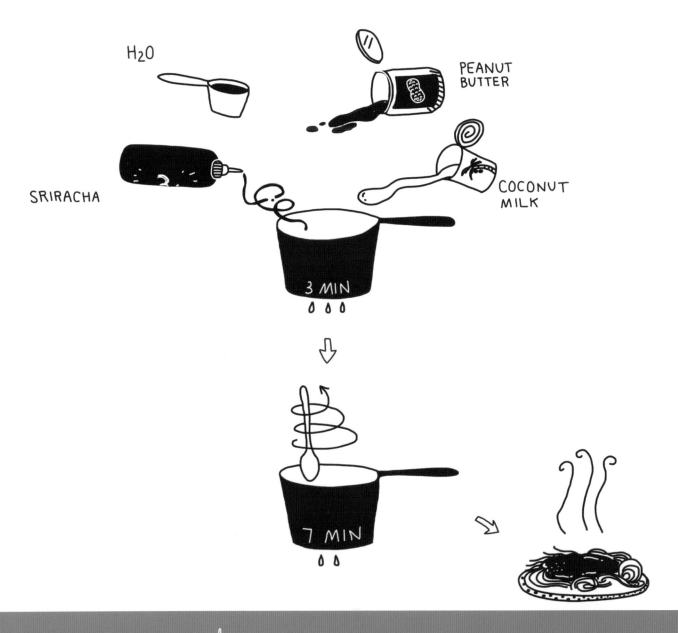

H₂O

PEANUT BUTTER

SRIRACHA

COCONUT MILK

3 MIN

7 MIN

 1 TBS SRIRACHA

 1 CUP H₂O

 3 TBS SMOOTH PEANUT BUTTER

 14 OZ COCONUT MILK

THOUGHTS ON RAITA

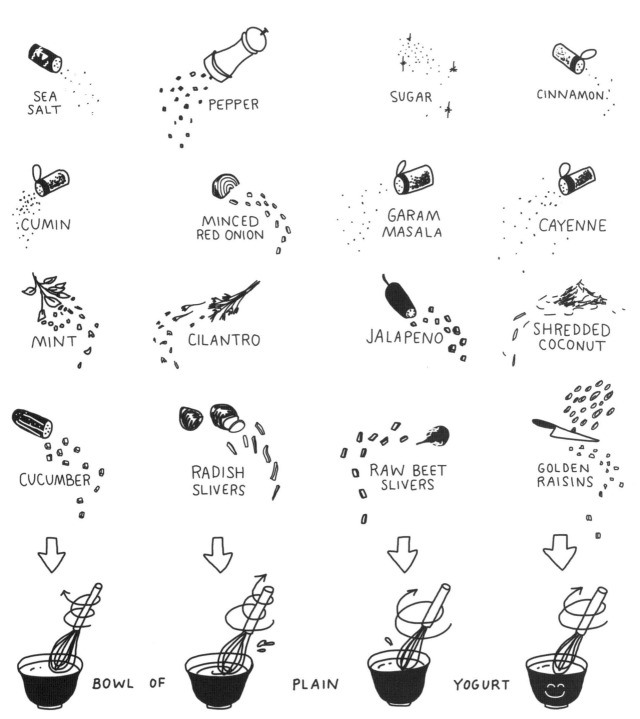

SEA SALT

PEPPER

SUGAR

CINNAMON

CUMIN

MINCED RED ONION

GARAM MASALA

CAYENNE

MINT

CILANTRO

JALAPENO

SHREDDED COCONUT

CUCUMBER

RADISH SLIVERS

RAW BEET SLIVERS

GOLDEN RAISINS

BOWL OF PLAIN YOGURT

DRINKS

GINGER TEA

BOIL
6 MIN

SIMMER
20 MIN

1 HAND
GINGER

ABOUT
7 CUPS H$_2$O

HONEY

ACTUAL CHAI

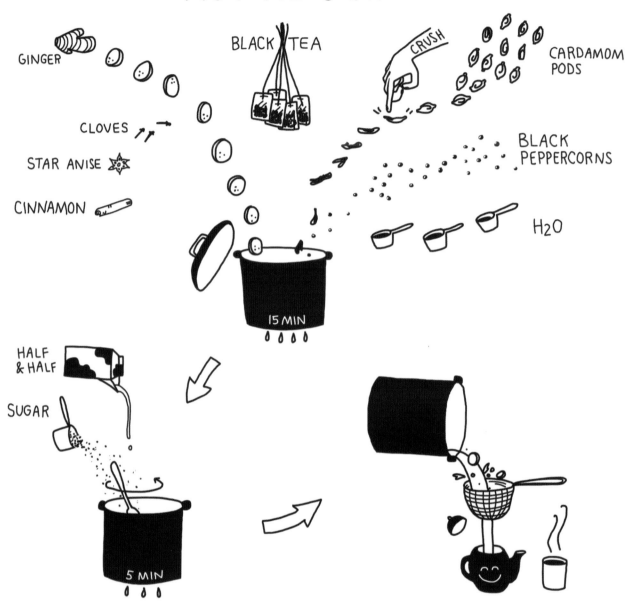

GINGER

BLACK TEA

CRUSH

CARDAMOM PODS

CLOVES

STAR ANISE

BLACK PEPPERCORNS

CINNAMON

H_2O

15 MIN

HALF & HALF

SUGAR

5 MIN

| 1 STICK CINNAMON | 1 STAR ANISE | 3 CLOVES | 1/2 HAND GINGER | ABOUT 5 BAGS BLACK TEA | BIG HANDFUL CARDAMOM PODS | 1 TBS WHOLE BLACK PEPPERCORNS | 3 CUPS H_2O | 2 CUPS HALF & HALF | 1/2 CUP SUGAR |

SUN TEA

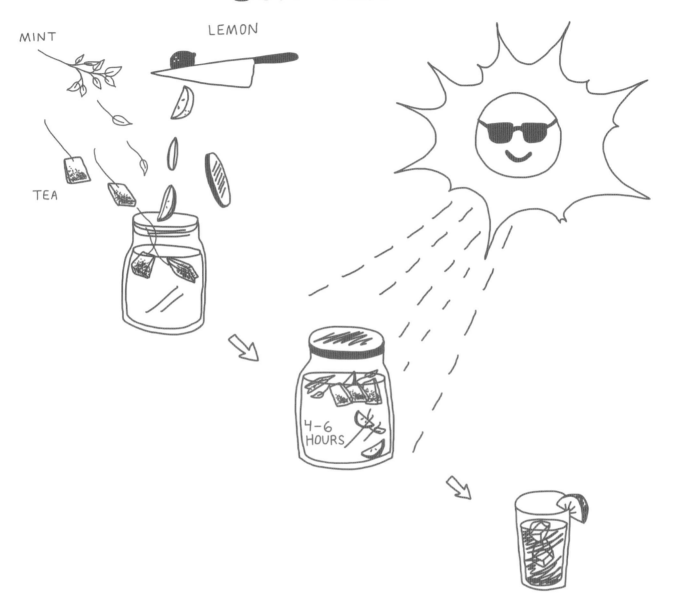

MINT

LEMON

TEA

4-6 HOURS

1 HOT SUMMER DAY

BIG JAR WITH LID, FILLED WITH H2O

3 TO 5 TEA BAGS

1 LEMON

1 SPRIG MINT

CLASSIC NYC EGG CREAM

MILK

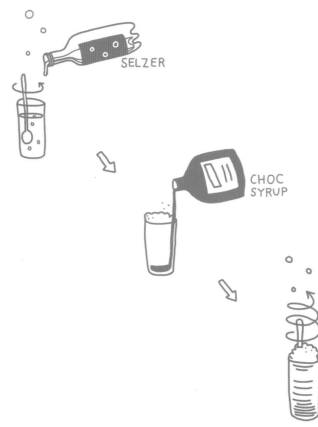

SELZER

CHOC
SYRUP

AN EGG CREAM CONTAINS
NO EGGS AND NO CREAM.

¼ GLASS
WHOLE MILK

½ GLASS
SELTZER

2 TBS
CHOCOLATE SYRUP

IMMORTALITY SMOOTHIE

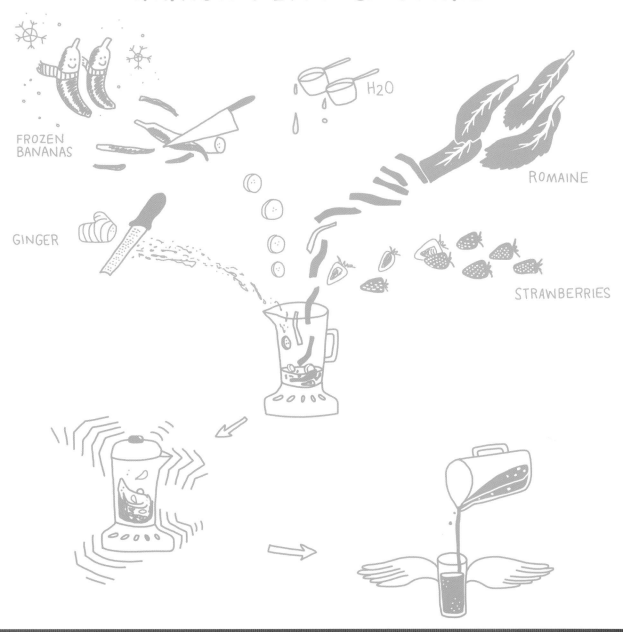

FROZEN BANANAS

H_2O

ROMAINE

GINGER

STRAWBERRIES

1 TBS GRATED FRESH GINGER

2 FROZEN BANANAS

2 CUPS H_2O

8-ISH LEAVES GREEN ROMAINE LETTUCE

HANDFUL STRAWBERRIES WITH STEMS

POP'S SMOOTHIE

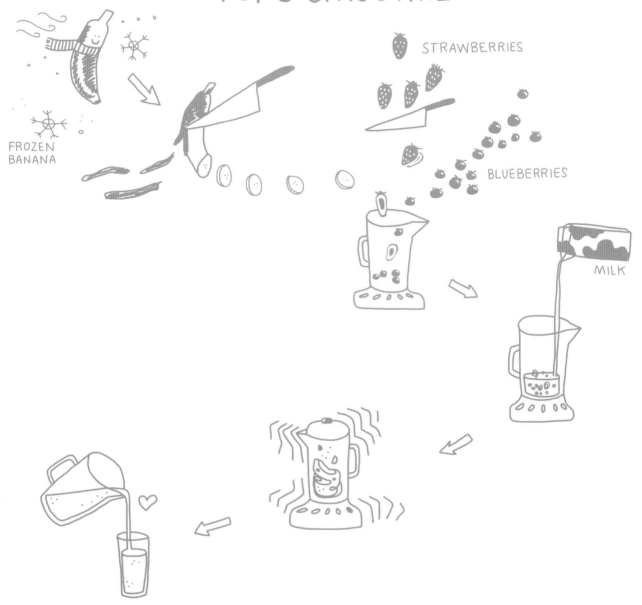

FROZEN BANANA

STRAWBERRIES

BLUEBERRIES

MILK

1 FROZEN BANANA

1 CUP STRAWBERRIES WITH STEMS

½ CUP BLUEBERRIES

2 CUPS MILK

DESSERT

STACEY'S BLUEBERRY COBBLER

SALT

BAKING POWDER

SUGAR

FLOUR

MILK

9"
PRE - GREASE

SUGAR

BLUEBERRIES

STRAWBERRIES

350°   55 MIN

RAISE RACK

ICE CREAM

PINCH SALT

1 TSP BAKING POWDER

3/4 CUP SUGAR, PLUS 1 TBS FOR SPRINKLIN'

3/4 CUP FLOUR

3/4 CUP SKIM MILK

2 CUPS STRAWBERRIES

2 CUPS BLUEBERRIES

VANILLA ICE CREAM

RUPERT'S CHOCOLATE CAKE

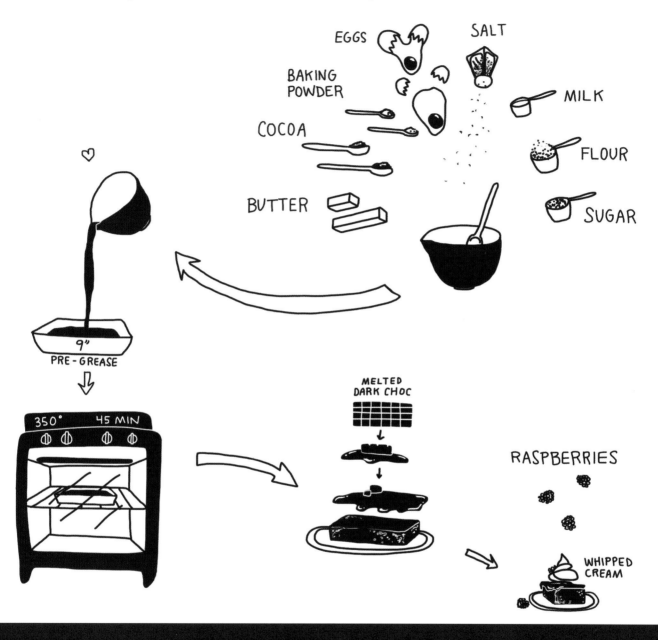

EGGS

SALT

BAKING POWDER

MILK

COCOA

FLOUR

BUTTER

SUGAR

9"
PRE-GREASE

350° 45 MIN

MELTED DARK CHOC

RASPBERRIES

WHIPPED CREAM

1 ½ STICKS BUTTER | 2 TBS COCOA POWDER | 2 TSP BAKING POWDER | 2 EGGS | PINCH SALT | 1 CUP MILK | 1 CUP FLOUR | 1 CUP SUGAR | DARK CHOCOLATE BAR, WHIPPED CREAM & RASPBERRIES

SWEET KUGEL

EGG NOODLE

TILL AL DENTE

RAISINS

APPLE

I STICK BUTTER

SUGAR

CINN

SALT

COTTAGE CHEESE

SOUR CREAM

I BAG EGG NOODLES

2 CUPS SOUR CREAM

1/4 CUP COTTAGE CHEESE

1 1/2 STICKS BUTTER

I CUP RAISINS

I GALA APPLE

½ STICK BUTTER

BROWN SUGAR

CORNFLAKES

CRUSH

350° 1 HOUR

¼ CUP WHITE SUGAR

1 TSP CINNAMON

1 TSP SALT

4 EGGS

½ CUP BROWN SUGAR

2 CUPS CORNFLAKES

CANDIED GINGER

GRANULATED SUGAR

20 MIN

COARSE SUGAR

SAVE THE GINGER SYRUP FOR SELTZER, TEA, PANCAKES...

DRY OVERNIGHT

POT OF GINGER TEA LEFTOVERS

REFILL POT WITH H2O

2 CUPS GRANULATED SUGAR

COATING OF COARSE SUGAR

GRACE'S KIWI PAVLOVA

EGG WHITES

SALT

ADD SUGAR 2TBS AT A TIME

MALT VINEGAR

GREASE TRAY

PILE HIGH

GAS OVEN

HEAT TO 450°
AND PUT IN
THE PAVLOVA.
TURN OFF OVEN
AND WAIT 90 MIN
WITHOUT PEEKING.

LET STAND

ELECTRIC OVEN

DON'T OPEN THE DOOR!!

HEAT TO 350°
AND PUT IN THE PAVLOVA.
WAIT 45 MIN,
THEN TURN OFF OVEN.
WAIT 45 MORE MIN.
NO PEEKING.

RASPBERRIES

KIWI

WHIPPED CREAM

 6 EGG WHITES

 PINCH SALT

 12 TBS SUGAR

 2 TBS MALT VINEGAR

 BUTTER

 2 HANDFULS RASPERRIES

 4 KIWIS

WHIPPED CREAM

BANANA BREAD

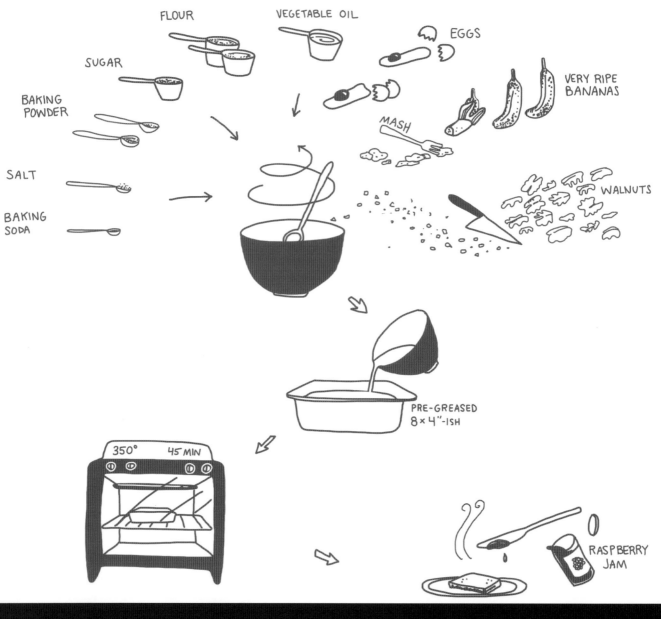

FLOUR

VEGETABLE OIL

EGGS

SUGAR

VERY RIPE BANANAS

BAKING POWDER

MASH

SALT

WALNUTS

BAKING SODA

PRE-GREASED 8 × 4"-ISH

350°   45 MIN

RASPBERRY JAM

 1/4 TSP BAKING SODA

 1/2 TSP SALT

 2 TSP BAKING POWDER

 2/3 CUP SUGAR

 1 3/4 CUPS FLOUR

 3/4 CUP VEGETABLE OIL

 2 EGGS

 3 VERY RIPE BANANAS

 1 CUP CHOPPED WALNUTS

 RASPBERRY JAM

AFFOGATO

CINNAMON

DARK CHOC

WALNUTS

SEA SALT

ALMONDS

ICE CREAM

ESPRESSO

 CINNAMON

 1/4 BAR DARK CHOCOLATE

 HANDFUL WALNUTS

 HANDFUL ALMONDS

 SEA SALT

 VANILLA ICE CREAM

 HOT ESPRESSO OR COFFEE

RICE PUDDING

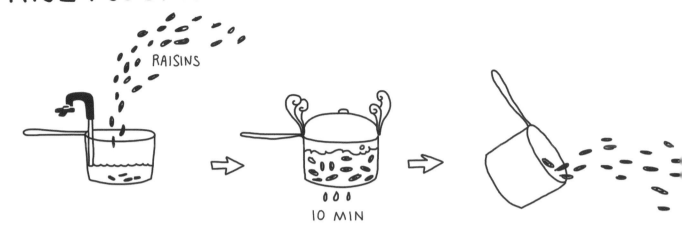

RAISINS

10 MIN

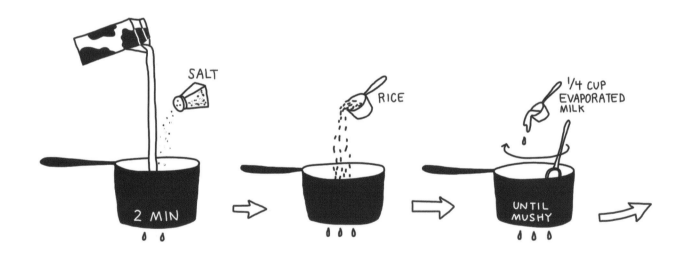

SALT

2 MIN

RICE

1/4 CUP
EVAPORATED
MILK

UNTIL
MUSHY

I CUP
RAISINS

1/2 POT H₂O

I QUART
MILK

PINCH
SALT

I CUP UNCOOKED
WHITE RICE

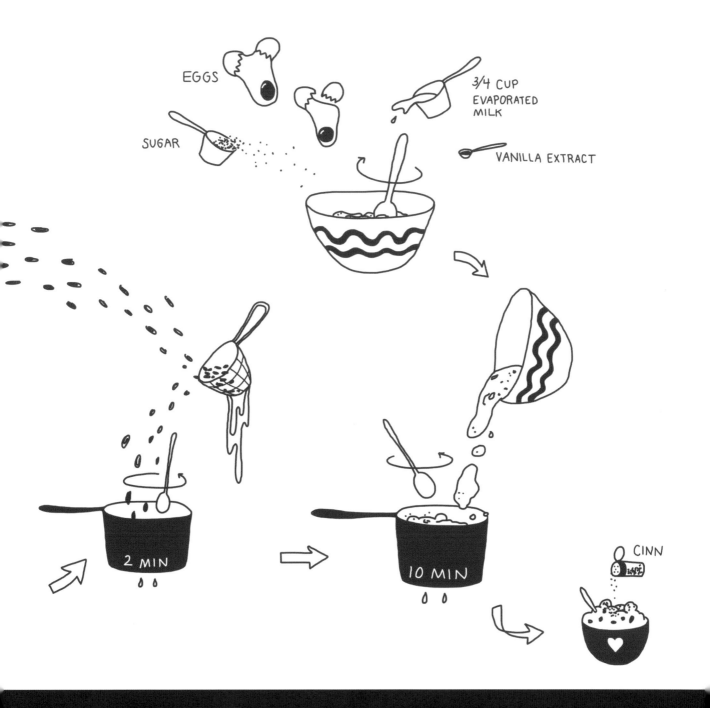

EGGS

SUGAR

3/4 CUP EVAPORATED MILK

VANILLA EXTRACT

2 MIN

10 MIN

CINN

½ CUP SUGAR

¼ CUP PLUS ¾ CUP EVAPORATED MILK

2 EGGS

1 TSP VANILLA EXTRACT

PINCH CINNAMON

INDEX

• VEGETARIAN RECIPES
• VEGAN RECIPES
• GLUTEN-FREE RECIPES
• DAIRY-FREE RECIPES
• NO SUGAR ADDED RECIPES

ABOUT THE AUTHOR

KATIE SHELLY IS A MEDIA DESIGNER AIMING TO MAKE YOUR LIFE SIMPLER, EASIER AND HAPPIER. SHE HOPES THAT YOU GET LOTS OF MILEAGE OUT OF THE RECIPES IN THIS BOOK AND THEY MAKE YOU AND YOUR LOVED ONES VERY HAPPY. KATIE WORKS AT THE COOPER HEWITT MUSEUM IN NEW YORK CITY AS A GRAPHICS

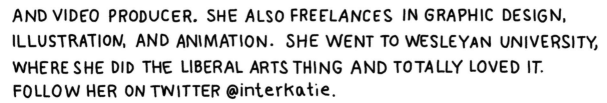

AND VIDEO PRODUCER. SHE ALSO FREELANCES IN GRAPHIC DESIGN, ILLUSTRATION, AND ANIMATION. SHE WENT TO WESLEYAN UNIVERSITY, WHERE SHE DID THE LIBERAL ARTS THING AND TOTALLY LOVED IT. FOLLOW HER ON TWITTER @interkatie.

KATIE WOULD LIKE TO SAY THANKS TO:

RECIPE·TESTERS
ALICE RIEGERT, AMANDA KESNER, BEN WEISGALL, BETTY FURMAN, DEENA SCHWARTZ, HANNAH HILES, KAITLIN KALL, MARIANNA SICILIANO LAUREN HARRISON & RUSSELL PERKINS

RECIPE-SHARERS
ANN SHELLY, ARIELLA THORNHILL, AURORA THORNHILL, BEN WEISGALL, CHERYL EDSON, CHELSEA WHITE, CHINO KIM, ELIZABETH MCCLELLAN, FRANCIS WEISS RABKIN, GRACE & RUPERT CHAN, JOSÉ CORTÉS VALENZUELA, KAITLIN KALL, KATE GAVRIEL, MARLO LONGLEY, NICK PERKINS, STACEY CUSHNER & TRAVIS FITZGERALD

ÜBER-HELPERS
ANNA WIENER, LEAH CAMPBELL, NICK FRIEDMAN, NICK PERKINS, PAM HORN, RUSSELL PERKINS & STACEY CUSHNER

AND OF COURSE
MOM & DAD, ANNIE & BILLY

A PORTION OF YOUR PURCHASE SUPPORTS JUST FOOD,
A NYC ORGANIZATION THAT CONNECTS LOCAL FARMS
WITH UNDERSERVED COMMUNITIES.

LEARN MORE AT JUSTFOOD.ORG.

HANDY METRIC CONVERSIONS

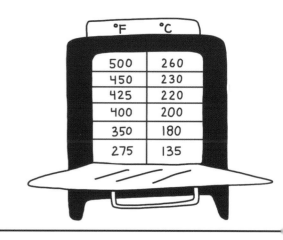

°F	°C
500	260
450	230
425	220
400	200
350	180
275	135

🌢 1 TSP WATER = 5 ml

🌢 1 TBS WATER = 15 ml

 ¼ CUP WATER = 60 ml

½ CUP WATER = 120 ml

1 CUP WATER = 240 ml

 1 CUP OATS = 85 g

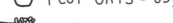 1 CUP RAW MUSHROOMS = 100 g

1 CUP WALNUTS = 128 g

1 CUP RAISINS = 165 g

 1 CUP COOKED RICE = 175 g

 1 CUP UNCOOKED RICE = 185 g

 1 TSP FLOUR = 3 g

1 TBS FLOUR = 9 g

1 CUP FLOUR = 150 g

 1 TSP SUGAR = 4 g

1 TBS SUGAR = 12 g

 1 CUP SUGAR = 200 g

2 oz = 57 g

7 oz = 198 g

24 oz = 680 g

32 oz = 907 g

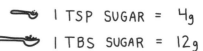

 1 STICK BUTTER = 114 g

 ½ LB = 227 g